A Will to Survive:
Ewa's Story

A Will to Survive:
Ewa's Story

Gill Turner

2011

ATHENA PRESS
LONDON

A Will to Survive:
Ewa's Story
Copyright © Gill Turner 2010

All Rights Reserved

No part of this book may be reproduced in any form
by photocopying or by any electronic or mechanical means,
including information storage or retrieval systems,
without permission in writing from both the copyright
owner and the publisher of this book.

ISBN 978 1 84748 887 9

First published 2010 by
ATHENA PRESS
Queen's House, 2 Holly Road
Twickenham TW1 4EG
United Kingdom

Printed for Athena Press

These memories are dedicated on behalf of my mother to her beloved husband, Bill, and to all of her family.

Author's Note

For all my life I have been aware of my mother's early years and the struggles she and her family had to face. Throughout the years snippets of information about this period in her life have been forthcoming and our family always said her story would make a wonderful book or maybe even a film.

It was only in later years, as my father's health deteriorated, that I decided my mother's story and the circumstances under which my parents first met, should be put to paper before it was too late. On starting this venture I came to realise I should have proceeded a lot earlier when my mother's memory was a lot sharper and more details could be gained.

My mother has never learned how to write in English so she recounted all she could remember and I made lots of notes and asked lots of questions. Some information was recorded onto a tape recorder so that I could keep rewinding until I was satisfied the facts were correct and made perfect sense. Once I had written each chapter I would read it back to my mother to ensure it was factually correct.

My main reason for writing this book is that I felt my mother's memories should not be forgotten and duly passed on to her family so they could come to understand just what she and many other Polish people had to endure in those awful times.

Acknowledgements

With thanks to my very special and much-loved mother, Ewa, without whom this book could not have been written. Without her strength and tenacity most of our family would not be here today. To my beloved father for his input and whom I miss every day, to Mietek for his memories and to Marysia for her assistance with the family fortunes. Also, to my dear husband, Mike, for his encouragement, typing and computer skills.

Preface

Prelude to the Invasion of Poland

In 1933, the National Socialist German Worker's Party, under its leader Adolf Hitler, came to power in Germany. Germany sought predominance of Europe, to take over Soviet Union territory and to eventually be surrounded by allied states, satellite or puppet states. Hitler's policy was to re-establish cordial relations with Poland while earlier working to weaken ties between France and Poland. His goal was to manoeuvre Poland into the Anti-Comintern Pact, forming a cooperative front against the Soviet Union. Poland would be granted territory of its own, to its Northeast, but the concession the Poles were expected to make meant that their homeland would become largely dependent on Germany, functioning as little more than a client state. The Poles feared that their independence would eventually be threatened altogether.

In addition to Soviet territory the National Socialists wanted to gain control of the 'Polish Corridor' and the city of Danzig. The Corridor was land disputed by Poland and Germany as it separated the German exclave of East Prussia from the rest of the Reich. By 1937 Germany increased its demands for Danzig and wanted a road built through the Corridor to connect East Prussia with Germany. Poland rejected this proposition as they distrusted Hitler which was fuelled by Germany's collaboration with anti-Polish Ukrainian Nationalists. The British were aware of the situation between Germany and Poland and on 31 March, Poland was backed by a guarantee from Britain and France that Polish territorial integrity would be defended with their support. The British Prime Minister, Neville Chamberlain and his Foreign Secretary, Lord Halifax, hoped to strike a deal with Hitler over Danzig and possibly the Polish Corridor so that war could be avoided and Germany would agree to leave the rest of Poland alone. Unfortunately the talks later broke down and for months there was no diplomatic interaction between Germany and Poland. In this period the Germans learned that France and Britain had failed to secure an alliance with the Soviet Union against Germany and that the Soviet Union was interested in an alliance with Germany against Poland. On 23 August after the discovery of secret Nazi-Soviet talks held in Moscow, Germany neutralised the possibility of Soviet opposition to a campaign against Poland and war became imminent. The Soviets agreed to aid Germany in the event of France or the United Kingdom going to war with Germany over Poland and in a secret pact they agreed to divide Eastern Europe, including Poland, with the Western third of Poland going to Germany and the Eastern two-thirds to the Soviet Union.

The German invasion was scheduled to begin on 26 August but was postponed until 1 September. This was because the Polish-British Common Defence Pact was signed with Britain committing itself to the defence of Poland, guaranteeing to preserve their independence. On 26 August Hitler tried to dissuade the British and French from interfering in the upcoming conflict, also thinking there was little chance the Western Allies would declare war on Germany.

On 29 August Germany issued one last diplomatic offer. This was the restoration of Danzig and the Polish Corridor in addition to safeguarding the German minority in Poland. The Germans were willing to commence negotiations but indicated that a Polish representative with the power to sign an agreement had to arrive in Berlin the next day while in the meantime it would draw up a set of proposals. On the night of August 30/31 a sixteen-point German proposal was read to the British Ambassador who requested a copy of the proposals was transmitted to the Polish Government. The German Foreign Minister, Joachim von Ribbentrop, refused on the grounds that the requested Polish representative had failed to arrive by midnight. When the Polish Ambassador, Lipski, went to see Ribbentrop later on 31 August to indicate that Poland was favourably disposed to negotiations he announced that he did not have the full power to sign, and

Ribbentrop dismissed him. It was then broadcast that Poland had rejected Germany's offer, and negotiations with Poland came to an end. Hitler issued orders for the invasion to commence soon afterwards.

The Invasion of Poland

The invasion of Poland by Germany, The Soviet Union and a small Slovak contingency marked the start of World War II. It began on 1 September 1939 and ended on 6 October that same year with Germany and the Soviet Union dividing and annexing the whole of Poland.

German forces invaded Poland from the North, South and West. As they advanced Polish forces withdrew from their forward base of operations close to the German-Polish border to establish lines of defence to the East. After the mid-September Polish defeat at the Battle of Bzura, the German's gained the advantage and Polish forces withdrew to the Southeast. Here they prepared for a long defence of the Romanian Bridgehead and awaited expected British and French support which in fact never came.

After the Soviet's Red Army's invasion on 17 September the Polish plan of defence was rendered obsolete.

Facing a second front, the Polish Government concluded the defence of the Romanian Bridgehead was no longer feasible and ordered an emergency evacuation of all troops to neutral Romania.

On the 6 October, the Soviet Union forces gained full control over Poland. The success of the invasion marked the end of the Second Polish Republic, even though Poland never formally surrendered.

On the 8 October, Germany directly annexed Western Poland and the former free city of Danzig and placed the remaining block of territory under administration of the newly established General Government. The Soviet Union immediately started a campaign of Sovietisation of the newly acquired areas. This included staged elections, the results of which were used to legitimise the Soviet Union's annexation of Eastern Poland.

In the aftermath of the invasion a collective of underground resistance organisations formed the Polish Underground State. Many of the military exiles that managed to escape Poland subsequently joined the Polish Armed Forces in the West, an armed force loyal to the Polish government in exile.

Introduction

My father, Grzagorz, was born in 1895 in Wilenszczyzna, Poland, at the time when the country was being partitioned by Russia, Germany and Austria. He was called up as a teenager to serve in the Russian Army and after serving for a short time, was posted to the Balkans and Greece. He was very disappointed at the lack of action and having come from a cooler climate he found it difficult to acclimatise to the higher temperatures. He left and made his way to France where he joined the French Foreign Legion. He was there for a couple of years, but on hearing news that Polish forces were amassing in France, he joined up with General Jozef Haller de Hallenburg's army, previously known as the Blue Army, because of the distinct French blue of the uniforms worn by its soldiers. It became known as Haller's Army after the General was appointed Commander and was accepted as the independent, allied and co-belligerent Polish army.

The Polish army was formed in France during the latter part of the World War I and, after the war ended in 1918, all the units were transferred to Poland where they fought in the Polish-Ukrainian and Polish-Bolshevik wars, fighting for the independence of Poland.

My father joined the cavalry. He served in the Krakus Unit and was duly issued with a horse, lance, sabre and rifle. He was awarded several medals, the most prestigious one being the Cross of Valour.

When the war was over, his detachment was located eighteen kilometres from the city of Rowne in a small village named Szubnow. It overlooked the Horyn Lake and the village population consisted mainly of Ukrainians.

He was given a room in a small farmhouse where a young girl and her father lived. The girl's name was Parakseda and she was the eldest with three younger brothers, Ostap, Kalenyk and Paulo, and a sister, Krysha. Their mother had died when they were all quite young so Parakseda was left to bring them up until they either left home or married. At the time my father moved in, Parakseda's siblings were all living nearby in the village and, as she was the last to leave, she still looked after her father, ran the house and helped out on the farm.

Many soldiers were stationed around the village and it was at this time that all the Polish army officers and soldiers who had fought for the independence of Poland were granted government land.

The land was divided up, forming three settlements: Jazlowce, Krachowce and Hallerowo. The latter was where my father was allocated his land. Now he had got his land, what on earth was he going to do with it? He realised he knew nothing at all about farming so he spent time deliberating which course of action would be best to take. He decided to ask for Parakseda's hand in marriage. He had witnessed first-hand that she would make a good wife and mother and was experienced at running a home and working on a farm. Her father, already knowledgeable on the subject, would also be of great help to him.

My father's offer of marriage was accepted and they were duly married.

Unbeknown to them, this marriage was to be sorely tested, but would stand fast and survive to last all their lifetime.

The Early Years

Now that my parents were married and my father had ownership of his land, the first thing they had to do was build a house. This was made of wood with a thatched roof and consisted of a kitchen, sitting/dining room and two bedrooms. A well was dug to supply water and an outside toilet was constructed by digging a hole and dropping a bucket down. A wooden box-like structure was built over this and a wooden toilet seat was secured on top. The bucket had to be regularly emptied and this job normally fell to Father as this was neither a popular nor pleasant task.

Sometime later, after completion of the house, my father, mother and her father moved in. They had brought horses and cows with them from the previous farm, so the first thing to do was to build a stable to house them. Next, the land was tilled so that crops of wheat, oats and barley could be grown. Luckily, the soil proved to be very fertile and good yields were forthcoming. An orchard was planted of apple and plum trees and beside the road leading to Rowne Tuczyn, cherry trees were grown. The last thing to be constructed was a barn to enable the grain to be stored for use, as and when they required it.

They surrounded all the buildings with a white picket fence and got themselves a large dog whom they named Burek. He was tethered by a long chain that ran from the stable to the barn. Ducks and geese followed and the yard became home to these and many chickens.

News that Mother had become pregnant was greeted with delight and I was born on 10 May 1923. I was followed a year later by my sister, Marysia. The year of my sister's birth was economically very hard as all basic goods were almost impossible to come by and wheat prices were at an all-time low.

Suddenly and without warning, Marysia died which devastated my parents and emotionally it was a very difficult time.

Two years of hard labour passed where my parents strived to

become self-sufficient – the farm being their only means of living and of earning any income. In that time, more additions to the family were forthcoming. In 1925 a daughter called Hanka was born, followed by their first son, Romek, in 1928 and a second son, Mietek, at the end of 1929.

My father still belonged to the Krakus unit and, along with many of the other settlers, was still involved in army training.

As the settlers married and time moved on, the number of children increased so it was decided that a schoolhouse was needed. Everyone that could help with the building got involved and it was constructed using bricks. It was also decided that a bakery and a dairy would be incorporated in the basement. The schoolhouse was to have a headmaster and five teachers: three women and two men. It also had a substantial sports field. A track was created that circled the boundary where activities such as skating, scout meetings and competitions could be staged. Finally, a shooting gallery was built alongside it.

Once again, my family expanded with the birth of yet another daughter in 1932 and it was decided to call her Marysia in memory of their second daughter.

As the farm matured, the livestock grew with the addition of pigs and all extra stock was sold at the local market. The sow, of course, was kept for breeding. This was a very lucrative time for us, but unfortunately, once we had a dozen pigs to sell, the price of pork suddenly plummeted. This dealt a severe financial blow, as it was an essential source of income. Father unfortunately became very stressed which subsequently caused him to lose some of his hair.

We would always kill one pig at Christmas time which was a great treat. It smelt and tasted delicious and what wasn't consumed would be salted down and kept in barrels to be eaten at a later date. The bladder was never wasted as Father made it into a ball for the boys to play football with.

We kept four horses, one of which was the cavalry horse my father rode in the war, and we used all of them for ploughing, etc. You could ride the cavalry horse, but you had to be very careful as he was trained to charge on certain sounds, music being one of them. One day, Romek decided to ride him and, as he did so, he cracked his whip. The horse took off at full gallop, thinking it to be a charge command, with Romek clinging to his back. Luckily, my father witnessed the whole thing and was able to shout out instructions to Romek. He thankfully survived but I don't think he ever rode that horse again.

We had three cows that supplied our milk and when they came into season they were taken to another farm to be serviced by a bull. When the cows gave birth, Father would kill the male calves for their meat and the females would be sold at the local market. We kept the cattle on a large field we owned, next to a wood. The field wasn't fenced and if any of the cows strayed into the wood and the ranger found them, a penalty was charged to get them back. Usually Grandfather would watch them or if any of the children were playing nearby they would keep an eye on them.

We also owned another field on the far side of the wood on which we used to grow grass to feed the animals throughout the winter. We cut it twice a year and it was stored in the barn for future use. The hay was also used to store apples after picking. The apples were put into boxes between layers of hay to protect them from frost, which gave them a longer storage life.

Some apples, along with plums and cherries, were dried by Mother in the oven and also kept for winter consumption when fresh fruit was no longer available. She also made wine from the morello cherries, which was well-known as father's medicine.

When it was time to gather the harvest I would help my father. We would cut it down with scythes and Mother would follow behind, gathering it into bundles. It would be threshed by hand to remove the grain and, when required, taken to the mill to be turned into flour. Sometimes, if we had enough money we were able to hire a mechanical harvester which saved days of hard work. Mother would always bake our bread on Saturdays and, if we could afford it, we would sometimes go on Sunday to the bakery to buy white bread as a special treat.

Due to a government incentive we were encouraged to grow sugar beet and tobacco. The sugar beets were harvested in October and we transported them to the refineries. As the tobacco had to be easily accessible for inspections, it was grown along the side of the road. It was deadheaded at the appropriate time and we harvested it in September. After cutting, the leaves were sorted into sizes and tied into bundles of twelve. Everybody helped; the children took the largest leaves, our parents the medium ones and Grandfather the crumpled ones. Having great patience, he would spend hours ironing them out to make them saleable. After being tied into bundles they were checked for mould every day before being sold. This was one of the highlights of the year as we were able to buy some much-needed clothes and shoes or items for the house. When the harvest was over, Mother would go off for several days to pick blueberries, some of which were made into a blueberry syrup. This was our medicine to settle an upset stomach. Mushrooms were sometimes available in the woods and I would go by myself to pick them and soon return with a basket full.

One day our dog, Burek, escaped from his leash and made his way into the forest. Mistaking him for a wolf, someone shot him, so he was replaced by a smaller black and white dog which we named Znajdek.

Our family expanded once more with the birth of a son, Bazil (whom Mother always called Vasik) and in 1937 another son, Janek, was born when Mother was forty-nine years old.

My mother was a small woman who was only about five feet tall. She had long dark-brown hair which she always kept plaited and secured in a circle at the back of her head. She wore long skirts and was always working. Now with six children and a farm to run she had little, if any, time to herself.

It was in the year that Janek was born that it was decided by popular consensus we needed to erect another church closer to the settlements, as the nearest one was about an hour away. Once again, anyone that could, helped, and slowly but surely the church was completed. It was named Matki Bozej Czestochowskiej and was situated in the Karlowszczyzna forest between Hallerowo and Krachowce. The church needed to be blessed and the Polish Lancers were invited to attend. They were a big draw and people came from all around to see them. They came from Rowno and carried the icon of the Virgin Mary into the church; her robe was adorned by crosses and medals of bravery that belonged to the settlers. Once the religious ceremony was over, everyone congregated outside the church and danced to music, courtesy of the local band. Vodka was freely available and a good time was had by all.

The pastor was to be Father Kakol. He was a young new priest and the son of a widow who lived in the settlement. Sadly, his brother, a pilot, was later killed in a plane crash and they buried him in the new church cemetery. The propeller was dismantled from his plane and set into his monument as a memorial.

Life continued and as we all got older we went to the local school, which was about one and a half miles away. Paths circled each farm upon which we were able to walk. I'd go with my friend Helka from our neighbouring farm and gradually we'd meet up with other children from the other farms. After school, when we got home, we would all do our homework before having set chores to do. All the children were given jobs and we thought nothing of it. It was part of our life and we were all expected to pull our weight. One of my jobs was to feed the ducks, geese and chickens. Afterwards, I would let them out of their pens so I could clean them out. The cows were also let out into the field to graze and were watched to prevent them from straying. I would sweep the floors in the hen house and do anything my mother asked me to do.

On bath night, which was once a week, I would help bathe my brothers and sisters. We had a tin bath which we put into the kitchen and the water was heated by a large boiler. Everyone went in, one after another, so if you were last you ended up with the coldest and dirtiest water.

I stayed at school until I was eleven years old. After that I was forced to leave because further education had to be paid for and unfortunately we didn't have the money as we didn't have a proper income. We were self-sufficient and lived off what we could produce. Another factor was that girls didn't need to be well educated as they were expected to get married and become wives and mothers. Once I had left school, I was required to help in the house and on the farm full-time.

As the family grew, my parents and grandfather decided to build an extra room attached to the then dining room to use as a bedroom for Hanka and myself. Initially, my parents shared one bedroom with the babies and the children shared the other. Hanka and I had beds, but the boys slept together on a wooden platform with a straw mattress. Now we were older and needed more privacy, the change was accomplished – much to the joy of my sister and me. It also gave the boys more room in their bedroom. Grandfather was no problem as he always slept on a wooden platform in the kitchen.

Several years passed and life carried on with everyone helping out, which of course saved us money as we didn't have to hire extra labour to help out on the farm. Plans were made for the future of the farm and the children's future. Maybe the boys could go to military school, etc. But it was not to be. Unbeknown to us, life would soon never be the same again.

Our World Falls Apart

I was around sixteen years old, it was the year 1939 and Poland was invaded by the Nazis on one side and by the Red Army on the other. As Father was still a member of the Krakus Unit he was once again called up to serve in the army. I was very proud of him and thought he was so brave as he would never hesitate when called to fight for his country. I knew he had been injured during the previous fighting as one leg was thinner than the other and his big toe was fused to the adjoining one. He had never spoken of his injury and, although we were curious, we knew better than to ask him about it. I can remember him getting all dressed up in his cavalry uniform, weapons at the ready and riding off on his faithful horse. It was a very tearful goodbye as we didn't know if we were ever going to see him again.

He was the mainstay in the running of the farm so if he was killed we wondered how we would be able to cope without him.

A few days later we heard the clip-clop of horses' hooves on the cobbled road and Father came into view. He had not been accepted by the commission and was bitterly disappointed, but the family was greatly relieved (although we tried not to show it too much).

One morning, Mother and I were out in the orchard picking apples when we heard an awful clatter in the distance and, as we listened, it seemed to be coming nearer and nearer. Feeling slightly alarmed, we returned to the house to find Father there; he had also come in from outside after hearing the noise. We all stood looking up the road. The sound became louder and louder until, all of a sudden, a column of soldiers came into view. Father's face turned white. 'Good God,' he said, 'it's the Russians, it's war, we've been invaded.'

We watched for days as columns of soldiers marched by, but they didn't have the appearance of a well-turned-out army. Some of the men were dressed in uniform, but not all – a large proportion were also dressed in civilian clothes. Many of their horses were thin and under equipped and quite a few of them weren't even fitted with a saddle.

Not every soldier owned a rifle so they came to our house demanding that Father give up his weapons as they knew he had been a member of the Krakus Unit. Fortunately, father had buried his rifle in a field for safe keeping and so told them he had been forced to hand it in after the war. He gave them his lance and sabre but also knew that if the rifle was discovered he would have been shot. For days and nights soldiers and tanks rolled on endlessly by.

A rumour was circulated by the Ukrainians that Szubkow was to be invaded by the Polish settlers. This was done in the hope that the Soviets would kill the Polish settlers and their families. No such event actually took place, but a lot of the settlers were forced to vacate their farms and Ukrainians were installed instead to look after and run them. Luckily, for the time being, we were allowed to stay on our farm. Contributing factors were that Mother and Grandfather were Ukrainian and, as we were such a large family, it would have been difficult to rehouse us elsewhere. A Ukrainian soldier was allocated to live with us instead and he was to oversee the strict rules we needed to abide by. He would stay with us all day but return to his house at night. We were requested to feed him and ask his permission to do anything, as we were informed that nothing was ours any more. We even needed to ask permission to kill a chicken for food. He stayed with us for several months as we carried on with our harvest and brought in the potato crop. The potatoes were put into small heaps and covered with straw for the winter. This was all carried out under his watchful eye.

On the night of 10 February, a date etched into our minds, we were woken up by a loud hammering on our door. Father got up from his bed and went to investigate. On opening the front door he saw a Soviet officer and several Ukrainians, all with red armbands, standing there. They pushed their way into the house and shouted, 'Get everyone up, we're taking you to another place; you don't need much, everything will be provided for you.'

Needless to say, panic ensued with everyone crying and not

knowing what to do next. Father was made to stand by a wall with his hands in the air, but luckily he kept calm and started issuing instructions. We got all the children out of bed and then dressed as fast as we could and started pushing things into sacks. Bedding, knives, forks, plates, whatever we could grab and think we might need. Mother gathered up any food that she could, dried pulses and fruit – in fact, anything we had – but unfortunately we didn't have any bread as it would have been her baking day the next morning. Most of our food was obtained straight from the field, orchard or livestock as and when we needed it, so there was very little to take with us. She dearly wanted to take a prized clock on the wall but the Soviet officer wouldn't let her. Anything valuable had to be left, including all our documents and what little money we possessed. We had a very short time to pack and all the time they were shouting at us, 'Hurry up, hurry up, we will give you everything you need.'

The worst thing that happened was we were told that as Grandfather was Ukrainian and too old, he wasn't able to come with us. It was heartbreaking to know that we would have to leave him behind, for as long as we could remember he had lived with us and was a pivotal member of the family. We would always remember him as being of medium height and sporting a grey beard and moustache. He wore white shirts which hung over his trousers and were pulled in at the waist by a belt. He was very kind to us all and he and Father would have big discussions about any decision that needed to be made. He could put his hand to anything and would make us bowls and spoons that he carved out of wood, flower garlands for his granddaughters and braided straw hats for his grandsons. For himself he made sandals out of willow twigs.

To know that her father couldn't come with us was so hard for my mother as her family was being ripped apart. She knew she might never see him or her sister and brothers again and she also didn't know what the future held for herself, her husband or her children.

We said our very tearful goodbyes to him, but we didn't have any idea what would become of him. We hoped he would be able to stay on the farm for a while to feed the animals, etc. before maybe going to live with his other children in the village as, like us, he would eventually be made homeless. Weeping and distressed we were ushered outside where two sleds were waiting. Two of our horses were tethered, one to each sled, and we hurriedly loaded our belongings onto them.

Half of us climbed aboard one sled and half onto the other and we set off on the road to Tarnopol, which was about fifteen miles away. For the whole journey our little dog Znajdek ran along beside the sleds, but we were not allowed to take him with us.

In those last few minutes we had lost everything we owned and had worked so hard for in all those previous years. As we continued, the journey became emotionally horrendous. After having been abruptly forced from our home and everything we knew, we had no idea what was to become of us.

On arrival at Tarnopol we were taken to the train station and saw the platforms were packed with settlers and their families, some of whom we recognised. We had to shoo Znajdek away and hoped he would return to our farm with the horses and sleds. We also noticed wooden trains were waiting, which resembled cattle trucks, and we were instructed which one to board, each one holding four families. On entering the 'carriage' we saw it was open in the centre and each side was divided up to make two floors by what resembled large wooden shelves coming out from either side. Two families, one being ours, went on the top sections, which were reached by wooden steps, and the remaining two families went underneath in the bottom sections. There was very little headroom so you could only sit or lie down. If you wanted to stand up you had to go to the centre of the carriage. The top floors had a small window you could see out of and a hole in the floor served as our latrine, which we later erected a blanket around to give some degree of privacy. In the middle of the carriage stood an iron wood-burning stove which was lit to provide some warmth – just about enough to stop us all from freezing. We were provided with absolutely nothing; no mattresses, no pillows, no blankets and no water.

We all huddled down together on the hard wooden floor, but luckily we had brought a few pillows of our own and a large goose down duvet which we snuggled under. Finally, the large wooden door was pulled across closing us in and the train started up, its *chug chugging* getting louder as it gathered speed. The sound of hysterical sobbing echoed around the carriages and was almost as loud as the train's engine. No one knew where our destination was to be, but in the morning, looking out of the window, the older people realised we were going to Siberia as we were travelling in a north-easterly direction. We didn't know it then, but we were to be in the train for about two weeks. There was nothing to do – just sit or lie around. Initially, the adults would talk to each other, but as the days passed the conversations died and everyone became quiet and withdrawn. The boredom, the discomfort, the cold, the hunger, the uncertainty was all consuming. Fear for the future gripped our stomachs as we wondered what was to become of us, were we going to survive?

The children cried a lot to begin with, but even they eventually went very quiet and would just look at you with big, sad eyes. They sat for most of the day on the top floor, looking out of the windows at the never-changing scenery. There was nothing but forests and everything was covered in snow that got deeper and deeper the further we travelled and the further we travelled the temperature got colder and colder. Occasionally, you might catch sight of a wooden dwelling but they were all boarded up and obviously deserted.

Each day the only thing we had to look forward to was when the train stopped to give us something to eat. During the day we had no food or water but the train stopped at night and some of the men were allowed off the train to get some fish soup and bread for each adult and child. They could also get water and some wood to keep the stove alight. There was no warning when the train was moving off again and we were always terrified that father would be left behind. About half an hour later, the train would come to a halt again, always in the middle of nowhere. Each night we had a knock on our carriage door and a soldier would ask if anyone was ill or had died. If the answer was in the affirmative, the door was opened and the sick were taken off and the bodies of the dead were laid out beside the track. Everyone in our carriage was all right, but when we looked out of our window we could see piles of straw and pieces of wood spread out on the banks nearby. We were all pretty certain that after the train had pulled out, the bodies of the dead were laid out and burnt. We feared that the ill were also killed and suffered the same fate as there was never a sign of any transport waiting to take them elsewhere.

The days passed mostly in silence; the adults realised the enormity of what was happening and feared for themselves and their children. We were all starving and freezing cold as the temperature dropped constantly the further north we travelled.

Poor Mietek was so thirsty he decided to lick the frost that had formed on one of the windows. As he did so his tongue stuck fast and as he pulled his head back to release it he ripped a large piece of skin off making his suffering even worse than before.

The toilet was hardly used at all as no one had enough to eat or drink to require it. We had no means of washing or keeping clean so we began to smell, but as we were all the same we didn't notice. We were still in the same clothes we had left our homes in but everything ceased to be important, keeping alive was the main priority.

Two weeks passed and eventually we passed the town of Kotlas and the train stopped at a village situated alongside the Dzwina River. Here we were taken off the train and shown to a large hall where we spent the night, once again on a hard wooden floor. In the morning we went outside to find sleds waiting and all the children were bundled into them. The adults were made to walk alongside, carrying their sacks, and we set off towards Archangielsk. As we trudged through the deep snow with no proper shoes on our feet, we became bitterly cold and even the river we were following was frozen.

Weak and exhausted, but much to our relief, we finally reached our destination.

A New Way of Life

On arrival, we got our first glimpse of what was to become our future home. The surrounding landscape was mainly forest, but in a clearing in the trees stood wooden log cabins. We were shown to one cabin, along with another family, with whom we were to share our accommodation.

As we entered, we noticed the inside was not very well furnished. It was completely bare in the centre of the room, save for an iron stove, and around the walls stood wooden bunk beds. We unpacked what little we had to make it more comfortable and lit the stove to provide us with some warmth. We were given some soup and bread to eat, then climbed into our beds to try and get some much-needed sleep.

The next day, everyone was kitted out with hard felt boots that resembled wellingtons and which hopefully were to prevent our feet from getting frostbite as the temperature outside was below freezing. We were also provided with a quilted coat, hat and gloves. Anyone who didn't possess socks wrapped their feet in rags to keep them warm.

The men and any boys over the age of eleven were given saws and axes and sent out into the forest to work. Their job was to cut down tall straight fir trees which were then passed to women who had the task of chopping off all the branches which were later burnt. Two or three men would then roll the stripped trees over into piles ready to be pulled to the railway tracks. The trees were finally transported by train to be used as railway sleepers or props for the mines.

Luckily, we had carte blanche to chop down as much wood as we needed to keep our stove alight, so at least we were able to keep reasonably warm once we were installed in our cabin.

We were only fed once a day in the evening and our meal consisted of mainly soup and bread. The Russian women gave us a few pulses if they had any to spare so sometimes we were able to boil them up for a little extra nourishment. Every day while everyone was working, Janek and the younger children were taken to a hall. There they were looked after by several Russian women.

Everyone was starving: you could visibly see the children's stomachs distending and the adults had lost substantial amounts of weight. Our clothes became filthy and gradually more and more ragged as they became caught and torn by the trees we worked with.

We obviously stank, but it never bothered us as we all smelled the same. After a time we ceased to notice it. We knew we all had lice as their bites made us itch and we were constantly scratching ourselves. If you looked very closely you were able to see the lice collecting in the seams of your garments.

There was a sink provided in a nearby dwelling which we could wash in if we wanted to. In reality no one did very much as no soap was provided and only ice-cold water was available. To strip off your clothes in a Siberian winter you probably risked hypothermia and freezing to death.

One day, my brother Mietek became very ill, but of course there were no doctors for hundreds of miles. Father deduced he may have caught pneumonia so Mietek remained in the cabin and was kept as warm as possible with hot water drinks. Father had heard that cupping glasses were supposed to help the condition. Made of glass, they are used as a therapeutic treatment for all sorts of illnesses. The glasses are heated up and then placed directly onto the skin. As they cool, a suction action is produced and blood is drawn to the surface. The purpose of these glasses is to rid the body of any impurities. With this in mind, my father went to call on all the other families in the camp to see if anyone possessed any. Luckily someone had some, which father was able to borrow and he used them on Mietek for two weeks. Gradually he began to feel better and, much to our relief, survived his ordeal.

Life in this camp was very hard. The freezing conditions and lack of food took its toll on everyone and survival became a daily battle. We stayed in the camp all winter and suddenly, out of the blue, just as the snow was starting to thaw, we were told we were moving on again.

It was May 1940 and, as fear gripped hearts and stomachs, we wondered if life could become any worse.

Life Struggles On

When we heard the news we were leaving, we proceeded to gather up what little belongings we had left. Our clothes were getting fewer and fewer as over the months they got more and more torn. Mother had, luckily, the foresight to bring a needle and thread with her when we left home so she was able to do some running repairs. Eventually, despite Mother's constant mending, some of our clothes became so ragged we could no longer wear them. We were told when our transport had arrived and subsequently loaded our things on-board. Although we didn't know where we were going, we were not sorry to be leaving this camp. We watched it disappear into the distance and waited to see where we were heading. Our transport turned out to be another cattle train and after boarding we wondered how many weeks we might have to endure this mode of transport. Much to our relief, we didn't travel too far and reached our destination later on that same day. We alighted, lifted our possessions onto sleds and were transported to the outskirts of a Russian village.

Our first impression on setting our eyes on our new home was that it had the appearance of a prison camp. We all found this somewhat alarming. The camp was surrounded by a high wooden fence and at the gate stood a watchman. A forest grew all around and, at each of the four corners of the camp, large lookout towers had been erected. As we were apprehensively herded through the gate, we saw lots of large wooden huts and a separate building. This building, we later learned, housed the toilets. They basically consisted of a hole in the ground with a wooden seat supported over the hole. This was, for us, indeed a luxury and gave us some degree of privacy when we needed to use them.

Every family was shown to a hut which would be shared with one other family, and we were allocated one half of the hut each. As we entered, we saw the hut contained very little in the way of furnishings. There were no mats or chairs, but both families had a stove they could use in the centre of the floor space. They provided us with some straw mattresses, pillows and blankets. We placed our mattresses together to make one large communal bed, as shared body heat was a good way of keeping warm.

We unpacked our belongings and tried to make the hut as comfortable as possible, as this was our new home for the time being. Later, we were shown to a church just outside the camp that had been converted into a canteen and given some soup and bread. Afterwards, we returned to our hut and snuggled down to sleep, wondering what the next day might bring.

On awakening, the men were ordered to assemble in front of the camp commandant. He had light hair, was stocky in appearance and seemed to give off the air of someone who was fair and approachable. The men were told that everyone old enough would be put to work and they would receive a small amount of money for their efforts.

In the main compound stood several large sheds, all housing lots of different types of machinery. This was where many of us would work and, once again, we would be dealing with timber. Father was given the task of finishing off wooden products such as beams, etc. and Mother and Hanka chopped wood for fuel to keep the furnaces alight. A lot of men were employed to chop down trees from the forest. After the trees were felled, the bark was removed by machine and the stripped trees were taken to the nearby river to be transported. The job of taking the trees to the river was tasked to several women, including myself. We achieved this by pushing a large pole beneath the tree and using it as a lever to roll it along the ground. This method was simple but efficient. On the bank near the water's edge, wooden props were angled and secured into the ground. The rolled trees were placed in a pile beside the props, and when the pile was large enough, the supporting props were knocked away. This caused the trees to fall into the water where they were then held close to the bank by several women using long poles with hooks attached to one end. Other women would stand on these floating trees and tie them together to form a raft. This was very dangerous work as the water close to the bank was very deep. Once a raft had been constructed it was pushed out into the centre of the river. There, a strong current took hold of it and the raft was carried off downstream to be retrieved further along. This was a good method of transporting the trees from one place to another.

One morning I awoke with a pain in my hand which slowly became worse and worse. My hand throbbed and the skin between my small and ring finger became badly swollen. I thought that this was due to the constant rubbing caused by the pole I worked with – the skin had broken and infection had set in. The pain became intolerable so I decided to take matters into my own hands. I pierced the skin between my fingers and, as I did so, a great deal of pus oozed out. Next, I cleaned the wound and applied potassium permanganate to disinfect it. This seemed to do the trick and my hand healed which was very lucky as we had no access to any doctors. In a medical emergency we had no backup; if anything happened you were on your own.

One terrible day one of the girls tying the trees together slipped and fell into the water in-between two of the floating trees and, as she disappeared, they closed back up over her. Whether she had hit her head or wasn't able to surface, we didn't know, but panic ensued as we desperately tried to find her. As the water was deep and very black we couldn't see so we shouted for some of the men who were working nearby to help. They rushed over, but no one could find her. When they eventually pulled her out of the water it was too late and she had drowned. That incident brought it home to me just how dangerous this work was and it was only by the grace of God that it wasn't me who had met this terrible fate.

Many months later I had the chance to change jobs. Being older, I was able to work alongside the men on the night shift, stripping the bark from the felled trees. The main reason I chose to do this was because you received more money than the day workers. I was issued with big thick gloves and would feed the trees through large saws which removed the bark. The tree was constantly turned and fed through again and again until all the bark had been removed. One day I saw blood everywhere and realised I had inadvertently sawn into my thumb. Luckily it was still attached!

All the work was supervised by Russian men. It was hard,

tiring work and not without its dangers. Concentration was vital if you didn't want to lose any fingers or maybe even an arm. Some of the trees were later sliced into sections and the older children sawed them into quarters and wheel-barrowed them up a hill for further processing. We worked six days a week and always looked forward to Sundays as that was our day off. While the adults were at work, the very young children were looked after by Russian women at a nursery school. Here at least they were given some much-needed milk to drink. The older children attended a school up until they became eleven years old and then they were put to work with the adults.

Every day after work we would make our way to the canteen in the church and be given our vegetable or fish soup and a portion of bread each. Occasionally, we had a change of diet and a stew was served up. There wasn't much meat in it and we believed the little there was to be goat flesh. We were constantly starving. Our stomachs had swollen and, having lost such a large amount of weight, we resembled skeletons. With the small amount of money we earned, and with the commandant's permission, we could leave the camp and walk to the nearby village. This village consisted mainly of women, the male population being only young lads and older men. The rest of the men had gone off to join the army, leaving their womenfolk behind to cope as best they could.

The local people didn't have very much themselves and were pretty poor, but they did have more than we did. With our pittance we could sometimes buy a few potatoes, some pulses or kasha (otherwise known as buckwheat. Mother used kasha to make soup and we bulked it out with any spare bread). Unfortunately with a family of eight to feed, the money wouldn't stretch very far. I made a conscious decision that we needed to supplement our diet somehow or some of us might not survive.

Mastering the Art of Foraging

The fence surrounding our camp was constructed of wooden planks and, after I had completed a reconnaissance lap of the boundaries, I found a place where one of the planks was loose. Being mostly skin and bones meant I had just enough room to squeeze myself through, enabling me to get to the outside of the camp undetected. Sometimes, if I was lucky, the guard wasn't present at the main gate which helped make my task a lot easier.

In the summer months, after a day's work, I would make sure no one was watching and I'd furtively sneak out of the camp. I headed off into the woods looking for wild blueberries and was delighted when I located some and picked them with gusto. I also became very adept at finding mushrooms. I worked out that the best way to spot them was to crouch very near to the ground and you would be able to see them sticking up. If you stood upright they disappeared into their surroundings, making them harder to find. Some of the mushrooms were huge and, on my return to the camp, Mother cooked them and we tucked into them with relish. We kept some of them on one side which were then dried to help sustain us through the winter months, as there was nothing to be picked in the woods once the snow set in. Any spare money we had was also kept for this same purpose.

My excursions always took place in the day as I worked on the night shift. I would wander through the trees and feel a great contentment. It was my way of escapism. Everything was so quiet and peaceful, you could push the hardships from your mind and find some sort of peace. Occasionally I would catch the sound of a Russian woman singing in the distance but I never managed to find out where the sound was coming from. Her voice created a haunting atmosphere and this contributed to making the woods seem even more magical.

Each time I made one of my trips I would explore new areas in the hope of finding something else we could eat. One day I couldn't believe my luck when I came across a farm that was growing fields of sweetcorn and potatoes. This was far too much for anyone to resist. A ditch ran alongside the field and, after looking very carefully one way then the other, to make sure no one was around, I dived into it. I then made my way into the middle of the field where I was certain I couldn't be seen and stuffed as many sweetcorn into my clothes as I possibly could, and headed in total joy for home. On future visits I equipped myself with rags and sacking so that I could carry as many as I was physically able.

The potatoes were also on my shopping list and I perfected the art of digging them up so as not to be detected. I scrapped the earth away with my hands, exposing the tubers, and picked them from underneath. I then replaced the soil so the plant itself remained undisturbed.

It never really crossed my mind the great risk I was taking. If I had been caught I would have been shot. When you're desperate you don't think of the dangers, you just do what you have to in order to make sure that yourself and your family don't starve.

One day, while out on one of my forages and investigating a new area, I suddenly came across a beautiful white church hidden among the trees. My curiosity got the better of me and I decided to have a closer look. It was very quiet and, after checking no one was around, I crept up to a window and peered through. I was shocked and horrified to see the condition of the church inside and the devastation that had occurred. Nothing of value remained and anything that was left behind was totally destroyed. The floor was literally covered in debris and broken items. I felt a great sadness that such a beautiful church could be desecrated in this brutal way, but learned later that this was very common and widespread under Stalin's rule.

Luckily I never felt any fear when going off on my own and was never afraid. Mother would never go as I think she worried that if anything happened to her, the family would not be able to cope. What she did take on herself though was to go begging for food in the village. We were not supposed to mix with the villagers but occasionally some of them would take pity on her and she returned with a few bits and pieces. Eventually we asked her to stop because we were worried she would get caught and be arrested.

On some of the times I went out I would observe an old Russian lady who seemed to live on her own. After a while we would wave to each other and one day she beckoned me over. She had grey hair, which she wore in a bun at the back of her head, and was dressed in a long skirt with an apron tied over the top. As I could speak some Russian we started chatting and she kindly invited me into her sparsely furnished home. I think she was lonely as this became a regular occurrence, usually on a Wednesday. She would give me a cup of tea and maybe a bit of bread and send me off with a handful of rice or pearl barley if she had any to spare. She didn't have very much, but she had a small garden where she was able to grow a few things. Every now and then she gave me a little salt or a small amount of soap, which was a great treat, as there was a widespread shortage of both these items. We became very close and I grew really fond of her; she was almost like a surrogate grandmother which was something I had never experienced before.

When we were having one of our regular chats, the old lady told me that my family were very fortunate when we had arrived at the camp as we had accommodation waiting for us. Apparently when she was young her grandparents and the rest of her family were moved under Stalin's rule and brought to the same area. They were provided with no shelter and were forced to build their own. A lot of the old people, plus many of the young, were unable to tolerate the cold and the hardships and so perished. She said a rumour had circulated that Stalin made soap out of the bodies of old people, but she didn't know if this was true or not. I noticed on my frequent visits that the house next door was empty and had been boarded up. This was something I had seen before on my trips outside the camp; I asked her if she knew why this was. She told me she had awoken one morning and the neighbours had just disappeared. She never heard what had happened to them, but this was to become quite common in a lot of areas as people were moved around under the new regime.

On some occasions when I sneaked out of the camp, instead of going to the woods, I headed for the river. Here I would usually find a pre-constructed raft, made out of thin wooden tree trunks, moored to the bank. I would jump onto it and, with a large pole, push the raft out into the river. This was quite a dangerous thing to do as this stretch of water was used by paddle steamers and once you got into the centre of the river it flowed very fast. Gradually using my pole I steered myself across the water to the bank on the other side, jumped out and made sure the raft was tightly secured. The last thing I needed was to be stranded and unable to get back. Once there I picked leaves, such as sorrel and on my return Mother used them to make soup.

One day a girl in the same camp as me was also using the raft to reach the other bank and forage when she fell off and into the water. No one was certain exactly what happened. It was thought that as she fell she got trapped underneath the raft and wasn't able to surface. Sometime later her body was discovered further down the river and retrieved. This episode made me very aware of the risk I was taking, but as the eldest, it was mainly down to me – and we needed to eat.

Making the Best of Things

One day one of my teeth started to ache and over the next few days it got progressively worse. My face became swollen and my mouth throbbed. My father realised I probably had an abscess, but as we had no access at all to doctors or dentists he decided to take matters into his own hands. He disappeared for a while and came back with a pair of pliers in his hands. 'Open wide,' he said and, with the pliers, gripped hold of the offending tooth, twisted it and pulled it out. I heard a scrunching sound and felt the pain, but it was short-lived and the relief to have the source of my agony removed superseded the discomfort of the extraction.

When we were forced from our home one of the belongings we managed to bring with us was a Bible. During the long evenings, and to pass the time, I would sit and read it and became very absorbed in its contents. I suppose I found out what religion was all about and received great comfort from this. I felt I began to develop a sixth sense and would dream of things at night which invariably came true. I found I knew when one of the girls in the camp was going to receive a letter. When I saw her I would tell her, 'You're going to get a letter soon.'

'How do you know?' the girl would say.

'I just do,' I would reply and, sure enough, not long afterwards she would receive one.

Something we were allowed to do in the camp was to write letters so Mother would write home to her relatives. Sometimes we received a letter back and occasionally they would send us a small packet which contained a piece of cured bacon or pork fat and maybe some kasha. This caused great celebration as we thought Christmas had come.

One morning we awoke to a letter sent to us from Mother's brother. He informed us that our home, along with all the other settlements that had housed the soldiers and their families, had been razed to the ground. Every single thing in each house had been stripped out, even hinges taken off doors, and transported back to Russia. Lorries laden with all our possessions, etc. had gone backwards and forwards day and night. Once everything that had a use had been taken, even the buildings had been destroyed, trees had been cut down and all the land cleared for communal farming. Anyone still left in the area was required to work full-time on the new government land.

We found this news heartbreaking. We thought about all the years it had taken to build our house and outbuildings, to plant all the trees and crops, and now they were all gone. It was a big blow to us all. Although we knew deep down it was unlikely we would ever see our home again, it had been a comfort to know that it was still there and there had always been a glimmer of hope that one day we might be able to return to it.

As our camp was quite close to the village, on Saturday nights some of the local lads would sneak in to see the young women. At first they were curious as to who we were. We were obviously not Russian, but we could speak a certain amount of the language. It also gave them an alternative place to go at the weekends. There didn't seem to be any romantic relationships struck up. They were always very polite and seemed to come for a good chat and the company. Even if a romantic encounter had taken place, pregnancy was never an issue as, due to the lack of food and the lifestyle we led, all the girls had stopped ovulating a long time ago.

One of the great highlights of our week was so-called bath night. This was held at the weekend and we all trooped along to one of the blocks where we were able to enjoy a wash in the luxury of hot water. Part of the floor had a dropped section which held several inches of water. In this we could paddle or, after washing, sit down and splash ourselves free of soap. It was heaven after what we had previously become accustomed to. While there it also gave us the chance to wash our clothes and, after they eventually dried, we would be able to wear them one week later.

The winters were bitterly cold and sometimes the temperature dropped to minus sixty centigrade. The thing we had to be very careful of was not getting frostbite. Hands, feet and noses were very susceptible, so Father kept a very strict eye on us all and luckily none of us succumbed to it.

Most of our shoes were very worn, or even worn out, so we would wrap our feet in whatever we could and then put them into bags. This helped to protect our feet and keep them warm, but they were very cumbersome when trying to walk.

Firewood wasn't readily available to us so it was a nightmare trying to stop ourselves from freezing. Some people had, in desperation, stolen some of the planks from the camp perimeter fence. For this crime the minimum punishment was to be locked up in a cold barn.

One day Mother, on her way home from the village, gathered up some twigs and small branches to burn in our stove. When she arrived at the camp gate the guard stopped her and she was charged with theft. She was locked in the barn for three days. This was our life as we knew it and we just carried on as usual.

Suddenly, in the month of July 1942, everyone was summoned to the hall by the camp commandant. Our fortunes were about to change once again.

Moving On

After receiving the summons, with some trepidation we all made our way to the hall to find the rest of the camp's occupants assembling. Half expecting to be made to listen to another Stalinist lecture, we went into complete shock with what the commandant had to tell us. We were to be freed in two days time. We couldn't believe it and the hall erupted in shouts of joy. People were hugging each other, some were sobbing, others were praying and some just stood in total disbelief. It was such a wonderful feeling it was hard to describe. Everyone started discussing where they would like to go, the most popular destination being somewhere much warmer. Suddenly reality set in. Here we were stuck in Siberia with no money and hardly any possessions so how on earth would we be able to realise our dreams? Little did we know we didn't really have a choice. After two years of living in the camp, we were informed we would be issued with documents and put on a train which would take us to Kotlas.

As we waited in anticipation for our departure the next two days seemed to take an eternity to pass. At last it was time to leave and each family was provided with a little money and enough bread to last them for three days. Our family received three loaves and Mother entrusted them to me for safe keeping. We were taken by truck to the train station and, once aboard the train, I placed the basket containing the precious bread underneath my seat and clasped it tightly between my legs. With emotions running high and being tired and hungry, I lapsed into a much-needed sleep.

Sometime later we decided to have our first meal. I opened the basket and, to my absolute horror, saw the bread had disappeared. Some unscrupulous person had stolen it as I'd slept. Father begged for the bread to be returned, as he had a family of eight to feed, but his pleas fell on deaf ears. We were totally distraught. The bread had been our only food for the next three days. Luckily, some compassionate passengers, who themselves had very little, shared their bread with us. For their act of kindness we shall be for ever grateful as this helped keep us alive.

During the journey boredom and hunger were once again the norm, but at least on this train we had seating, unlike on the cattle trains we had previously used.

Days later, tired and weak from the lack of food, we finally arrived in Kotlas. Here we found a Polish Organisation that helped us. We were only here for a short time when we were once again put on a train which was heading south. Hunger, yet again, became the main issue and although we still had a little money remaining, it proved to be worthless to buy food. Nobody wanted money; it had no value and no one would accept it. The Soviet rouble was even being rolled up to make cigarettes. People were only interested in trading food for goods which were in short supply.

After several days of travelling, we arrived at the city of Andziezan. Father told us to get off the train and, on alighting, we patiently waited for his instructions. He told us to wait beside a fence and then he promptly disappeared. We were all panicking as we didn't know what was happening, but he eventually reappeared and told us to follow him. He proceeded to lead us to an area where horses stood tethered to two-wheeled buggies. We loaded our possessions on-board the buggies and climbed on. We never found out how father had managed to arrange this mode of transport as he always kept everything to himself and neither of us dared to ask him. He could speak fluent Russian so whether he received help from the Polish organisation in Kotlas or anyone else remained a mystery, but we were greatly relieved to be finally off the train.

We travelled for several hours to reach our destination, which was a commune named Stalin. On arrival we were given some bread and water and shown to our new accommodation. This turned out to be one of two mud huts situated on the outskirts of the local village. The hut was very basic. It had a mud floor, a cooking stove with a saucepan, one straw mattress and one chair. Being the head of the family, Father had the use of the chair and the mattress. The rest of us were given straw to sleep on and we had to eat all our meals sitting on the floor. The huts were surrounded by fields used for growing a variety of crops. On seeing these our eyes lit up. There were fields of vegetables such as beets, sweetcorn, tomatoes, marrows and potatoes, most of which we hadn't seen or tasted for a very long time.

Father was given a cleaning job at the local airport and the rest of us were put to work in the fields. Some of our duties consisted of weeding or helping to gather the crops and whatever else was demanded of us.

For food we were provided with chapattis and flour from which mother became a dab hand at making pasta. As an added bonus she was given permission to gather a certain amount of beets and tomatoes for our own consumption. Of course, this still wasn't enough to satisfy a family of eight so I took it upon myself to supplement our diet.

Our hut was quite close to the toilets. Each toilet consisted of a hole in the ground, topped by a wooden plank, also with a hole cut into it. Little did we know that this was to be one of our life's luxuries. Beside the toilets ran a wooden fence with a convenient gap in it. This enabled me to squeeze through the fence and, hidden by the toilets, I could make my way to the fields undetected. What choice did I have? Mother would tell me what to pick and off I'd go, obviously extremely careful not to be seen. Being able to have the extra food, we began recovering from our arduous journey and felt that life was beginning to improve.

Unfortunately this wasn't meant to last. After little more than a week our luck ran out once again.

Father was working at the airport when he was stopped by an NKVD (police) officer who asked to see his papers. On presentation of these documents, the officer decided they were not in order and Father was escorted back to the commune. We were ordered to collect our belongings and then were taken to the station where we boarded another train. Its destination was unknown. The train was made up of twelve wagons and each housed several toilets. We were allocated one wooden bench and a hammock, which was positioned above it, for all the family's use. As there were so many of us we had no choice but to take turns in sleeping. Every now and then the train would stop and a little bread and water, or sometimes a bit of pasta was dished up for us to eat.

Father realised the train was heading south and, as we continued, we crossed the Volga River. This was the widest river I had ever seen in my life. We carried on towards Moscow, passing through the outskirts and our impression was that Moscow looked like a vast and beautiful city. To pass the time we spent hours looking out of the windows. We noticed dozens of army vehicles moving about and organised chaos seemed to ensue everywhere. We surmised that the army was being mobilised to fight the war against Germany. One thing we also learned was that we were the only people on the train who were not Polish Jews!

After several days of travelling we arrived at the city of Dzalabat in Uzbekistan. Once there no one seemed to know where we were supposed to go. We were left on the train all day, under the watchful eye of the NKVD, and when night fell the train set off again.

We had no idea where we were heading, but later learned that it was Andziezan. Once we had arrived here, the train turned around after a short time and went back from where we had come. This continued for three days going back and forth. No one knew what to do with a train full of Polish Jews.

Food was scarce and we were gradually starving. Fortunately, Mother had the foresight to bring a few beets with her from the previous farm. Although they didn't fill us up they at least kept us going. At last the train stopped once again at Dzalabat and the doors finally opened. To everyone's relief we were allowed to get off the train, but by this time a lot of the occupants were in a very poor state.

Our family was singled out. We had no idea what was to happen to the rest of the unfortunate passengers and we didn't get a chance to find out. We were escorted to a nearby square where lots of other people were milling around. Horses and carts were standing nearby and everyone there was divided up into groups and allocated a cart. We piled our meagre belongings on-board, climbed up, and the horse trotted off. Sometime later our new destination came into view. It was another commune named Stalin.

A Nightmare in Cotton

As we arrived at the communal farm the first thing we saw was a village of mud huts. These were occupied by the Uzbek locals, but there were two huts situated slightly apart from all of the others. We were given one of them and the family that had accompanied us was given the other. This family consisted of a man and his wife, his sister-in-law and his three daughters. Over time we were to become good friends with them.

Once inside our new accommodation we could have a good look around. The floor and walls were made of hardened mud and in the middle stood a cooking stove with a few saucepans on top. There was a large stack of straw piled high on one side that we spread out to make our sleeping quarters. This straw, we later learned, was changed every so often. No toilets were provided. When nature called we went outside and used the fields, finding cover where possible and using the softest vegetation at hand for toilet paper. To wash we used the local stream. This was also used to wash our clothes and for our drinking water.

Father was quickly given a job to do. His task was to look after the horses, but found most were sadly in a truly pitiful condition. His other duties included mucking out the stables and keeping them clean. The surrounding area of the village consisted of vast fields of cotton. The cotton needed to be regularly picked and this is what all the elder members of the family were assigned to do. The youngest three went to a school in the village. We were provided with large cotton sacks and went along the rows of growing plants, picking the cotton and filling our sacks. When they were full, we carried them to waiting lorries and they were taken away. Equipping ourselves with another sack, we carried on picking cotton, repeating the process over and over again. It was very hot and tiring work. We worked all day long, stopping only for an hour to eat lunch. This was always chapattis washed down with water. By the end of the week we were exhausted. The heat,

The Big Sergeant:
William (Bill) *Albert Pitcher*

Bill (centre) and co-workers of the Repair and Salvage Unit

Me, Ewa Ludwiga Cisalowicz

Me working at the MOT Section

With best friend Anela

Bill's father, William Pitcher, as a sapper in World War I

Bill's Mother, Alice Elizabeth Pitcher (nee Bodenehr)

Our wedding, 2 April 1944

Main wedding party

Our wedding cake

A happily married couple

Second Avenue, Acton. Bill's grandparents on balcony

22 Newburgh Road, Acton (on left-hand side)

My three angels: Linda, Marilyn and Gill, from left to right

Me, Linda, Marilyn and Gill at Newburgh Road

Rumble Weir, Willowbank

The River Colne at the bottom of our garden

Gill at 32 Coast Road, Pevensey Bay

Our fiftieth wedding anniversary, 1994

My three angels at our fiftieth wedding anniversary

Our sixtieth wedding anniversary, 2004

Telegram from the Queen

Me (centre) with my six grandchildren, Jason; Mark; Chris; Lianne; Lisa and Kieren, and Chris's new wife, Nic

Me with ten of my twelve great-grandchildren

Romek as a paramedic

Mietek

Hanka

Marysia

Janek and me

A family visit to Eastmoor Camp, York, with my father (standing in the centre, first row) and my mother (standing third from the right)

long hours and meagre diet took its toll and we were glad when the weekend came around – not that we had long to recover as we only received one day off a week. We were not paid for our work, but father did receive a little money for his.

After all the cotton had been harvested, the fields were ploughed over ready for planting for the next year. Once the tractor had finished its task lots of large clods of earth remained behind. Our job was to walk up and down the fields and use sticks and rakes to manually break them up. Another thing we had to do was to level the ground. If we found any hollows we shovelled soil into a structure that resembled a stretcher. This was carried by two of us to transport the soil to where it was needed, then tipped into the hollow and the ground levelled. We were always given something to do, we were never left idle.

Food was scarce in this camp and we became hungrier than we'd ever been before. A major drawback was that there were no woods or anything growing in the near vicinity where I could scavenge for edibles to supplement our diet. Father was able to obtain a little milk now and again and this was given to the children. Occasionally, he brought home some goat meat or horse meat, which was popular, and some flour. He also managed to get his hands on some pearl barley and dried peas from the farm, which we presumed he had to pay for.

The terrain we were living on was extremely hot and dry. Other than the cotton fields, the surrounding areas were craggy and the ground was covered in rocks so nothing was able to grow on it.

One piece of information we received was that small tortoises lived up among the higher ground. We learned these were regularly caught and eaten by the local community. I decided we would follow suit and, armed with a piece of sacking, I set off. I walked for some time; the ground rose and became rockier under my bare feet. I had no trouble in spotting the tortoises. They were small and round and obviously not hard to catch as they couldn't move very fast. I filled up my sack and, when I couldn't carry any more, I set off for home. I didn't enjoy catching these reptiles and, on my return, I gave them to Mother to deal with. One of the local women showed my mother how to kill them. This she did secretly when none of us were around. I believe they were then boiled in hot water to remove them from their shells, skinned, cut up and cooked. We were grateful for the meat, but didn't want to know how it was prepared. I made several trips and on two of them was once accompanied by Mietek and once by Marysia.

Being able to get enough food for us to eat was becoming a real problem. One morning a dog appeared. He was old and thin and hung around our hut for several days. Suddenly he disappeared, and the older ones among us noticed that we had a different meat added to our diet! Unknown to us, and under the cover of darkness, Father had caught and killed him. He was skinned, chopped into pieces, wrapped in a cloth and hidden in the base of our stove. We needed to consume the meat as quickly as possible because in the intense heat it would have soon gone off. The locals had seen the dog and realised that it was no longer around. They guessed what had happened and, thinking we were Russian, laughed and called us Russian dog eaters. Mother and I were aware of what Father had done but we kept it to ourselves.

One tree that grew in the area was an apricot tree. Unfortunately, the fruit on these trees was out of reach to us as we had no means of being able to pick them. After the local villagers had eaten the apricots, they spat the stones onto the ground and these could be found everywhere. We would retrieve the stones, break them open and eat the kernels inside. We didn't realise that in excess these could be dangerous, but we obviously never ate enough to do us any harm.

Although we lived on the outskirts of their village, the locals were friendly towards us. Their womenfolk wore long dresses and had shawls draped around their shoulders. The men wore trousers with long coats. Their lengthy hair was styled into a large plait which hung down the centre of their backs.

One day I met one of the younger men and he asked me if I would like to go to his house and have a meal with him and his mother. This was a very tempting offer as the thought of extra food was a great attraction. I agreed as long as my sister Hanka could go with me. That evening we rather nervously made our way to his hut and were invited inside. The interior was not that different to our own place and the only difference was that there were mats on the floor and straw mattresses to sleep on. On the stove stood a large pot, not unlike a wok, in which his mother had cooked meat and rice. She placed the pan in the centre of the mat area and we all sat cross-legged on the floor around it, dipping into the pan with our fingers. We ate its contents with relish. Once we had finished, we said thank you and set off to return home, accompanied by our male host. As I walked beside him, I suddenly got a shock when he started pinching my bottom. *What on earth is he doing?* I thought to myself and promptly swapped sides, putting Hanka between myself and him. Undaunted, he came and walked beside me again. When we arrived home he made a beeline for Father and engaged him in conversation. It suddenly dawned on us all that he wanted to marry me or, at the very least, buy me as a wife. He began offering goods in exchange for me: a goat, sacks of apricots, etc. and as Father kept saying no, he offered even more goods. He must have thought Father was driving a hard bargain. Mother saw what was happening and although she was small, she was feisty. She jumped in and said, 'No, no,' and much to my relief ushered him as quickly as possible out of the door.

Afterwards I realised that he had pinched my bottom because he thought it was either a sign of courtship or he wanted to feel what he was getting. After this episode I saw very little of him and carried on as usual.

Sadness and Hope

My little brother Vasik was the second-youngest member of the family. He was a lovable and lively child with brown hair and big blue eyes. Always mischievous and highly inquisitive, he was full of life. One day, as usual, he went off to play with some of the other children. Later on that same day he became ill with a high temperature, frequent vomiting and diarrhoea. Over the next two days he became progressively worse. We surmised it was probably a gastric problem, but as we had no access to doctors and he was too ill to move, there was very little we could do. Mother took him into bed with her so she could look after him the best she could, but when she awoke in the morning she found him lying dead beside her, having passed away in the night. Afterwards she found out from the other children that while out playing, Vasik was so hungry he had eaten what he thought were small cucumbers. They obviously weren't edible and unfortunately they must have been poisonous. He was around seven years old. The whole family was totally distraught and we would miss him terribly.

Mother was too upset to do what was necessary so it fell to me to lay him out and wash his small, painfully thin body. I found the best clothes that he owned and gently dressed him in them. Still reeling from the shock, we realised that because of the intense heat, we needed to bury him as quickly as possible. Father disappeared and came back with a pile of thin planks of wood. He set to work making a small coffin and a simple wooden cross. While Father was busy, Vasik's siblings went into the fields and returned with bunches of wild flowers.

Once the coffin was completed, we carefully laid Vasik inside. Father enlisted the help of the man who lived in the next hut to ours and together they picked up the coffin and started walking towards the higher ground away from the camp. The rest of the family followed behind.

Nobody spoke and the silence was broken only by the sound of sobbing. We continued on for about a mile, climbing slowly upwards until we reached a stream. Nearby ran a path and on one side we saw lots of mounds which we believed was the local cemetery. As we watched, the men laboriously dug a grave on the other side of the path, making it very deep to avoid jackals that frequented the area from digging it up.

When the hole was finished, we lowered the coffin gently inside and covered it in the removed earth. Father set the wooden cross he'd made at the head of the grave and the children laid their wild flowers on the top. The man's wife, who had also accompanied us, was quite a religious person. She said some prayers and we all sang some hymns. It was very hard to leave, but in a sombre mood we made our way back to the village. Through force of circumstances we were only to visit the grave one more time.

Not long after burying Vasik, Hanka and Mietek became ill. Fearing the same thing could happen to them, we knew we needed to take them to hospital. This was the best part of a morning's walk as the hospital was in the town of Dzalabat. Father, Mother and I decided it needed to be done so we set off, walking very slowly and carrying them if necessary. Finally, hours later, hot, tired and thirsty we arrived at the hospital. After the doctors had examined Hanka and Mietek they informed us that they both needed to be admitted as they were suffering from dysentery. We were forced to leave them and they stayed in the hospital for two weeks. They were not given any medication, just sour milk to drink. While we were in Dzalabat we learned from some soldiers that there was a Polish Social Services Bureau in the town. On hearing this news we made our way there, registered and were allotted some bread. On returning home, Mother sliced the bread thinly and dried it in the sun to preserve it.

Every other day for a fortnight, Mother and I made the journey to the hospital, taking some of the bread with us. We would pass it to Hanka and Mietek through the hospital window. Although they were given some food, it was very little, so they looked forward to the chat and extra provisions with anticipation. Luckily, the cotton-picking season was over which therefore enabled us to make the frequent visits. If the season had been in full flow we wouldn't have been able to visit the hospital at all. At last the two weeks were up and, much to our relief, they both seemed to have made a full recovery so we were able to bring them home.

The events of the past few weeks began to play on my mind and I realised that we would never have a future in this godforsaken place. One by one we would gradually die. We were always hungry as we never had enough to eat and we had little hope of ever leaving. I became so desperate I knew I had to do something about our situation. My sixth sense kicked in and I felt I had to go into town. I spoke to my parents about my feelings. I said that if we stayed where we were things would never improve, we would have no future, and none of us would come out alive.

I was adamant that I was going into town whether Father agreed with me or not. He was worried about me going off on my own, but could see I wasn't about to change my mind so he gave his consent. As luck would have it there wasn't much work around so I was less likely to have been missed. If anyone asked where I was he was to say I was ill.

The next morning I got up bright and early, so no one would see me, and set off towards the town with no food or water, just determination. The road into town was a large dirt road that ran through the mountains. The terrain was mostly scrub with large rocks dotted around and the atmosphere was hot and dry. It would take me most of the morning to reach my destination which I undertook barefoot. I met a few people on the way, also on foot and the odd horse and cart would pass by. I wasn't really afraid of being on my own, but I did have a fear of being raped. It was so isolated with not many people in the near vicinity. Luckily, my fears were never founded and I safely arrived in the town. Here I found a pump where I was able to get a drink of water to quench my considerable thirst.

In the centre of the town was a market square which contained a few stalls selling various produce. There were a lot of people milling around and, as I mingled with them, I realised they were speaking Polish. This was the first Polish I had heard being spoken for some time and my spirits lifted. I walked among them for a while, trying to listen to what they were saying so I could ascertain why they were all there. In the end I decided to stop two women and asked them outright what was happening. They told me they were waiting to get some bread. A British Red Cross lorry was due to arrive soon and it would be dispensing loaves to those who needed them. I saw a queue was beginning to form so I joined the end of it. Eventually a large lorry drove up with three men on-board and stopped at the start of the queue. The men got out and opened up the back of the lorry and started issuing out the bread. Slowly the queue got shorter and shorter and finally I reached the front. One of the men asked me how many members were in my family. I was given one and a half loaves and one small bit. I was so happy I would be able to take this extra food home. Being very hungry I ate the small piece of bread which was my breakfast and lunch combined.

While standing in the queue I was behind two men who seemed very excited and kept talking about 'Great Britannia'. I realised they meant Great Britain which is where the lorry had come from. I needed to know what they were talking about. I took a deep breath, excused myself and asked them the reason for all the excitement. 'Oh,' they said, 'we've just joined the Polish Army. Have you got any brothers?'

'Oh yes,' I replied, 'I've got two.' They didn't ask me what ages they were so I didn't volunteer the information.

'That's good,' they replied, 'if you go down the road on the right you'll see a big white building with the door open. Go inside and you'll find two Polish Officers, see them and they'll tell you what to do.'

'Thank you very much,' I said.

After I had received my bread, I walked to the corner of the road as directed and there I saw the white building. Apprehensively, I approached the door and, as I peered in, I saw the two officers seated inside. I was very nervous as I knew my brothers weren't old enough to join up and I would have to lie about their ages.

I walked up to them. They seemed very nice and asked me to sit down. They started asking me questions about where we were staying, about the rest of my family and what ages my brothers were. 'One's nearly eighteen and the other one's sixteen, approaching seventeen,' I lied.

I sensed they knew I was lying and my brothers weren't old enough to enlist but I didn't let that deter me, I just kept talking.

I explained to them the conditions under which we were living, the past tragic events and if we had to stay there none of us would survive.

'That's all right,' they said, 'go back and bring all your family here tomorrow morning and stay by that wall. We are waiting for transport to arrive, it could come tomorrow, it could come next week, we don't know for certain, but you must wait there,' and again they pointed out the wall where we should wait.

'Great Britannia' was mentioned again, but I wasn't sure if the aforementioned transport had anything to do with the British Red Cross or not.

I could have kissed the officers! 'Thank you so much,' I said and made a beeline for the door. On the way home I didn't walk, I literally flew. I ran as fast as my legs would carry me until I arrived back where my anxious parents were waiting for me.

I recounted the day's events to them and what the officers had told me. I could see by their faces that they were scared and worried.

'We've got to go,' I said, 'it's our one chance to get out of here; if we stay we will all die.'

It was a massive risk for them to take, to leave some sort of life for we knew not what, just on the information I had imparted. After a discussion I felt very proud that my parents trusted me enough to decide we would go.

We spent that evening gathering together what little belongings we possessed. It wasn't much: a few clothes, a bit of food, anything else we could carry which would be of some use to us and then we sat and waited for midnight.

After checking outside that the coast was clear, we crept silently out of our hut and started walking in the direction of the town.

It was slow progress and took us all night to reach our destination. Everyone was tired and weary and it had been a marathon task for all the younger children as they would have normally been asleep in bed.

As morning dawned we made our way to the wall that I'd earlier been told to wait beside. Many other people had already started to gather there. Some of these were families from the surrounding areas and, as luck would have it, we found ourselves close to an army canteen. Soldiers were inside having their breakfast and the smells penetrating the outside made our mouths water. After the soldiers had finished eating, some of them came out with a large pot of porridge and proceeded to dish some out to us. Boy, did it taste good!

We stayed in the area for a few days and the British Red Cross, who ran the canteen, fed us for this time. Mainly, the food consisted of bread and soup or chapattis and anything they were able to provide. We finally got word that the last transport would be leaving the train station at midnight so everyone made their way to where the train was waiting.

A large crowd of people of many different nationalities, including some Jews, had showed up, all in the desperate hope of being able to board the train. Unfortunately, many did not have the correct documentation and were not allowed to board. When our turn came we breathed a large sigh of relief as we were allowed to get on.

We were so thankful to have escaped our past hard life, but we had no idea now if we had jumped from the frying pan into the fire or what the future had in store for us all.

A Persian Paradise

We climbed aboard the train and were very relieved to find it was a passenger train with reasonably comfortable seats and toilets. After the type of transport we had previously been used to, this was luxury indeed. We had no idea where our final destination was to be but hoped it wouldn't be any worse than the earlier ordeals we had suffered. One other good thing was that we were provided with some food which was usually bread and soup or a type of sandwich.

We travelled for several days with nothing to do but sleep or look out of the windows at the changing scenery. The train came to a halt at Krasnowodzk, beside the Caspian Sea.

We gathered our belongings together and alighted the train. We were told to wait on the quayside for a boat to take us on the next leg of our journey. We waited for some time without any food or water being provided. Eventually, a small freighter docked alongside and we all climbed aboard. Food, once again, wasn't forthcoming, but luckily we had a few crackers left which sustained us through the voyage. These had been given to us by the soldiers before we had left.

At last, the freighter headed inland and it anchored two kilometres from the shore of Pachlewie in Persia. We were transferred into several motorboats and taken to a camp situated by the sea.

On first arrival we were ushered into the communal baths. Here everyone had a thorough wash and it was absolute heaven. Unfortunately, we were all covered in lice so all the men and boys had to have their heads shaved. The women and girls' hair was cut very short and treated with a solution that smelt like paraffin. Any clothes we had, plus most of our possessions, were taken away and burnt. As it was hot the children were given bathing suits to wear. Later on, as Hanka and I were sitting around, a man walked past us and, as he did so, looked at us both, then at our bare feet. 'Come with me,' he said. We dutifully followed him and he led us to a door which he proceeded to unlock. It was obviously a storeroom because as we entered, we saw a large pile of clothes and lots of black plimsolls in the middle of the room. 'See what you can find,' he said.

My and Hanka's eyes lit up. We hadn't worn anything on our feet for months, so without hesitation we dived into the pile of plimsolls and started sorting out pairs for all the family. Next, the clothes, but unfortunately they mostly consisted of underwear and nightwear. On seeing some nightdresses, I had an idea. If we cut down the arms, shortened the hem and made a belt out of the material we'd cut off, we would have a dress. Mother had a needle and cotton, which she had brought with her from our old home so with this idea in mind we sorted through the clothes. I chose a blue nightdress for mother and me and Hanka picked a pink one dotted with flowers for herself. When we had finished we thanked the man very much and left excitedly with our chosen items. We lost no time in putting our plan into action and once the garments were finished, we put them on straight away. We felt like a million dollars – a dress and some shoes! What more could we want.

As it was a hot climate the sleeping quarters were on the beach. We slept on the sand under a lean-to which was like a tent but with open sides. Each of us was given two different coloured blankets.

We were fed three times a day from a communal kitchen which included lamb and rice. Not a bowl of soup in sight. It was fantastic!

We'd spent years eating mostly soup. Our stomachs were not used to having so much food and those who overate ended up in the camp hospital with sickness and diarrhoea. Being in this camp was like being on holiday. We had no work to do so spent most of our time sitting and relaxing on the beach or going for a swim or a paddle. The children loved it as they could go in and out of the water as many times as they wanted and never needed to dress or undress. Their costumes dried very quickly in the intense heat. One day some soldiers gave us our first taste of Fray Bentos corned beef. We thought it was absolutely delicious but I must have eaten too much one time as I spent a couple of days feeling sick and unwell.

Romek suddenly took it into his head that he wanted to join the army cadets. Soon after though, he unexpectedly went down with jaundice and ended up in the camp hospital so that failed to materialise.

One day, out of the blue, we spotted an old face from the past. It turned out to be Mrs Lepucka, a neighbour from our home settlement – Hallerowo. She and her husband had two sons and a daughter, and when we were forced from our homes, they were put on a different train to us. It was great to see someone from our past life, but when she told us her harrowing story we realised just how lucky we had been.

As we listened intently, she told us that when travelling they had been given salty fish to eat, which consequently made them all very thirsty. They were given no water to drink and then the train suddenly came to a stop in the middle of nowhere. There was a nearby stream and they were told they could drink as much as they wanted there. What they weren't told was that the water was contaminated, so unknowingly they drank heartily. The result was that lots of people got dysentery or typhoid, which proceeded to spread rapidly among them and many died. She sadly lost all her family. Father realised Mrs Lepucka wasn't well and insisted she went with him to the camp hospital. Unfortunately it was too late to save her and she died shortly afterwards.

We stayed at this camp for several weeks and were gradually putting on weight and our health was improving. This was living the good life. After all the hardships we'd endured before we revelled in the knowledge that we were fed three times a day and were also not required to work.

Unfortunately our time here was short-lived.

Life Gets Better

Once again, as had happened many times before, we were told we had to be moved on. We collected our belongings together and loaded them onto the waiting trucks. These drove us to a place named Achwas at the foot of some mountains. Here we were housed in a large school hall which was overseen by a commandant. The food was reasonable and was cooked by the local women. Sometimes they gave us home-made macaroni, cooked in milk, which was a very pleasant change to our diet. There was nothing to do so we just whiled away our time doing nothing. This was to last for a couple of weeks until more trucks appeared and we were on the move again. These transported us to another camp based in Tehran where we found our life was to change for the better.

On arrival, we received some new clothes and were offered a more varied and wholesome menu. School classes were organised for the children, but unfortunately no notebooks were available. The adults basically had nothing to do so we were left to amuse ourselves.

We got the impression that nobody knew what to do with us. We appeared to be in a transit camp. During the time we were here, we were able to regain our strength and put on some much-needed weight.

After approximately three months we were put back on trucks and driven to the docks where we boarded a waiting passenger ship. We had no proper sleeping quarters, but were given the run of the upper decks. This was where we were to spend our time and also sleep on the wooden floor. We were well-fed with three meals a day which was great and something we were now getting used to. On-board there was a general blackout as U-boats operated in the area. Mines in the water were also a constant threat.

In the event of an emergency situation we were given

instructions telling us what we needed to do. We did have one scare when a vessel was spotted nearby. All the women and children were gathered together and placed strategically around the deck area as a decoy. This, thankfully, worked and so what could have been a disaster was averted.

The journey seemed long and boring as there was nothing to do and nothing to look at other than mile after mile of endless ocean.

A small relief was that after two weeks we docked at Bombay in India to unload some cargo. On completion of this task we set sail again and finally reached our destination of Karachi in Pakistan the next day.

We disembarked and were met by Red Cross nurses. They escorted us to a camp in the desert on the outskirts of the city. A barbed wire fence ran around the perimeter of the camp which contained many large tents. Everyone was accommodated in these, around four families per tent. Camp beds were provided, which was a great luxury to us as we usually slept on the floor. We were given a very good diet and also pocket money in keeping with the English custom. We settled in very well here and felt quite happy as we were well looked after and could do very much as we pleased. The only restriction was that we were not allowed to leave the camp compound.

Stationed nearby was a division of Polish soldiers who were allowed to visit our camp at the weekends. They were required to report to the gate on their arrival and departure. Their visits were the highlight of the week, and were eagerly awaited by all the young women. Initially, the soldiers came to see if they could recognise anyone, but after that it was to laugh and flirt with the women, who were only too pleased to comply. Everyone would talk together and go for walks in the camp grounds and generally have a good time. It was something to look forward to as there was nothing else for anyone to do so it came as a welcome relief.

One night as I lay sleeping I experienced a very vivid dream about my grandfather, whom we had been forced to leave behind. I dreamed I was standing in the garden of my home in Poland and coming towards me, holding hands, was my grandfather and Vasik, who was also no longer with us. As they approached,

Grandfather gave me a message to pass on to my mother. 'Tell her—' he said. 'Yes, I will,' I replied, but when I awoke I couldn't remember what he had said. When I saw Mother in the morning I said to her, 'Grandfather is dead.'

'How do you know?' she replied, so I recounted my dream to her. Several days later we received a letter from one of Mother's relatives. Grandfather had been shot and killed. He had been working out in a field when he had spotted some German soldiers coming along the road in his direction. Having made a beeline for the woods nearby to hide, he was seen by the soldiers and shot while trying to escape. The family were very upset to hear this sad news. He had lived with us and had played a very large part in our lives – he would always hold a special place in our hearts.

Christmas came around and all the children were given sweets, dolls and toys which made it feel like the real thing. However, not long after we heard we were to be moved on once again.

Our journey was suddenly delayed as Mietek contracted malaria. This enabled us to stay on in the camp a bit longer. Shortly afterwards, Marysia also became ill. We were not sure exactly what was wrong with her so she was taken to the hospital in Karachi. Mother decided to stay with her and they were there for over a week. When Marysia was finally allowed home she had lost nearly all of her hair. It had been originally straight, but as it started to grow again it came through curly. Once she and Mietek were fully recovered, we and our belongings were put on to trucks and driven back to the docks. Here we boarded a freighter whose destination, we were told, was Africa.

Because no one in my family could speak or understand English, I never knew the reason why the British Red Cross moved us on from one place to another. I assume it was either for safety reasons or because of the large amount of needy people they had to deal with.

Life Continues to Improve

Once on-board the freighter, we found that a deck was to be our living quarters. Here we slept, ate and entertained ourselves. We had brought the blankets and pillows we possessed with us so did our best to make ourselves as comfortable as possible on the hard wooden flooring. This served as our mattress.

We were fed three times a day but as this wasn't a passenger ship, no entertainment of any sort was provided. Our days were spent walking the decks or looking out to sea at the never-changing view. Occasionally some dolphins were spotted, which caused great excitement and helped break the monotony. The days passed very slowly.

It was to take four weeks before we reached our destination. For most of this time, everyone was on edge as we knew our ship was sailing through very dangerous waters.

The waters were patrolled regularly by German U-boats and for this reason there was a general blackout. One day this danger was brought home to us when another freighter was observed shadowing ours. We had an army on-board so orders were issued for them to be hidden out of sight while all the women and children were gathered together. We were placed to one side of the ship, as had happened before, so when the following freighter caught up with ours all their crew were able to see was women and children. The ploy worked and thankfully it passed by without challenging us. It was a very scary time and we all heaved a sigh of relief when it was over.

At long last, land was sighted and we docked at the port of Mombasa. This was the first time any of us had encountered black people. It was an unfamiliar experience for us. Although we felt a little wary at first, they also held a fascination as they looked so different to what we had previously been used to.

We were taken to a train and, as we set off, naked children with their arms outstretched ran alongside, begging us to throw them something to eat. This was the first time, since we had been forced from our home, that we had observed others worse off than ourselves. It tugged at our heartstrings, but we had nothing we could give them.

The next two hundred miles of travel took us through the Kenyan countryside. This consisted of scrubland with a lot of sand and the odd scattering of trees.

Eventually, the train drew to a halt near a camp called Masindi, close to the town of the same name. Tired and dusty, we alighted and took in our new surroundings. There was a very large jungle clearing and within it stood mud huts with roofs made of elephant grass and a hole in the centre for ventilation purposes. We were shown to a hut and, on entering, found it contained camp beds, blankets, pillows, a stove and saucepans. We were held here for a week, during which we were given medical examinations to determine the state of our health before being transferred to another village.

Here we were given linen, clothes and cork hats to protect us from the scorching sun. The tropical sun was something we were not accustomed to and it took us quite a while to acclimatise. Every so often we went to see a nurse who would check our bodies for places where *jigger flies* may have burrowed. These were tropical fleas, the fertile female of which would burrow underneath the skin and lay her eggs. This caused an intense irritation which could become severely infected. Favourite places for them to burrow would be around finger- and toenails. If you found one, you would have to put up with the discomfort until the area came up to form a type of small sac. Only then would the nurse burst it and remove the flea from inside. You could try to do this yourself, but it left you more susceptible to infection. *Jigger flies* were very common and proved to be a real nuisance.

Food wasn't a problem here as we were able to obtain it from a stockroom and Mother would cook it on the stove outside our hut. Gardens were established and people planted tropical fruit such as bananas, papayas and pineapples.

The children went to school from eight o'clock in the morning until two o'clock in the afternoon. Scouts clubs were also formed for out-of-school activities.

Places of work were available for the adults. You were given a choice of carpentry, sewing, brick-making or making footwear. We were paid a small amount of money for our labour and the good thing was that it gave us something to do with our time.

Hanka and I decided we would like to have a go at brick-making. We dug the clay out of a clay pit, situated just outside the village, and put it into wooden troughs. We then added water and mixed the clay with a shovel until it was of the right consistency before transferring it into moulds. The moulds were placed in the sun and left to dry until the clay was hard enough for them to be turned out. The bricks were then put into storage and, when enough had been made, were used to build a church and a hospital.

If we wanted to spend any of our wages we were able to visit the next village where you could purchase a few things. Our pay was very meagre and to get to the village you needed to go through a jungle area. We were informed that elephants frequented this area and could be dangerous, so I thought better of it and never made the journey.

I made several friends during this time and one of my best friends was a girl named Anela who lived in the adjacent hut. She was a single girl on her own and lived with another family group. She had chosen to help the nurses, either removing *jigger flies* or doing whatever else was needed.

One day, the village received news that young women were being asked to volunteer to join the Women's Polish Army. They were to be based in Nairobi and the army requested them to help sew parachutes. The packing of these and of dinghies was also needed. On hearing this news I thought this might make an exciting change from our jungle way of life. I spoke to Anela about it and she agreed with me so we put our names down to volunteer along with about sixty of the other young women. Although I would miss my family, I had no qualms about leaving them as I knew they were being fed and were well looked after. I would also be able to write to them and they were still near enough for me to visit.

Everyone that could, wanted to help the war effort so my parents accepted my decision, although they were obviously upset to see me go. It was several weeks before confirmation came through that we'd been accepted. After a tearful goodbye, Anela and I boarded the train bound for Nairobi to start a new chapter in our lives.

Striking Out Alone

As we sat on the train, Anela and I were filled with a mixture of excitement and apprehension as we didn't quite know what we had volunteered for. Later that same day, the train arrived at the station in Nairobi and, as we alighted, we were shown to several waiting trucks. These took us to an open camp just outside the airport, which was about five miles from the town. The camp was made up of large wooden barracks constructed in lines. Once inside we were allocated a bed, which turned out to be very comfortable, pillows and blankets. Each of us was issued with a khaki uniform with the word 'POLAND' on the lapel. We had a communal wash house where we were able to shower and where we could also wash our clothes. The camp was overseen by a Polish woman commandant, Eugenia Jaworowska, but was under the jurisdiction of the British Royal Air Force. Half a mile away from our camp was an RAF camp named Eastleigh and nearby stood several large hangers. These were where we would be working.

Every morning we donned our overalls, ate breakfast (which consisted of bread, cheese and coffee) and, in formation, marched off to work.

Some girls were given the task of repairing or packing parachutes and dinghies and I was allocated to the MOT section. This was where any vehicles that had sustained substantial damage or had broken down were brought to be repaired. The whole operation was overseen by the RAF and a lot of our co-workers were Indian or black people.

On our first day, we were shown what had to be done by several of the men who already worked there. They were full of smiles and a lot of eyeing up was going on between us. The men thought it was great to suddenly have all these single women around. We girls were also very happy to have these available men around too.

We worked on large tables in the hangers. We were given a part of a vehicle, shown how to fix it and when it was mended, given another part. Lunchtime lasted one hour. We ate the sandwiches we had brought with us and sat and chatted with the men. Obviously, there was a lot of laughter and flirting going on as everyone was lonely. We had only just started learning English so we had to communicate the best that we could. The conversations contained some Polish, some English and some Swahili, but despite that we seemed to make ourselves understood. When our shift was over, the girls gathered on the parade ground and marched back to the camp, being eyed up by the RAF men as they went.

In the week our evenings were spent mainly in our barracks which housed around twelve girls each. We spent most of our time chatting to each other as there was no other entertainment.

The weekend was the highlight as there was always a dance held in the camp on Saturday night. In the daytime, straight after breakfast, we often caught the bus into Nairobi.

It didn't take long for a lot of the girls to get English boyfriends. Mine was a motorbike courier named Roger. He was really nice and we would often visit the Stanley Hotel for a cup of tea or coffee. Afterwards we would go for a walk or sometimes watch a film at the local cinema. A lot of courting was going on between the Polish girls and the RAF men. This even applied to the married ones who had wives back home. The popular consensus was to live for today and what people didn't know wouldn't hurt them. Contraceptives were readily available so some couples would sneak off to the woods and reappear some time later. There was a curfew so everyone had to be back at the camp by eight o'clock in the evening.

I went out with Roger for a while but as I met him one day he seemed to be very upset. He informed me that he had been posted to Egypt. We were unable to do anything about this so we said our goodbyes and he left.

After Roger had gone another chap, Jimmy Talbot, who had shown an interest in me, asked me out. He worked in the parachute packing hanger and told me his family owned a well-known shoe factory back in Britain. I didn't find him that attractive but I thought it's no good sitting on my own in the camp so I agreed to go out with him. We went to the cinema in Nairobi, but after we'd had a few more dates I found he wasn't really my type so I ended the relationship.

While away I kept in regular contact with my family by sending letters and exchanging photographs. Now and again I caught the train back to Masindi and I would spend a week visiting them. They were always very pleased to see me and seemed happy and content. Not long after I'd left, Romek enlisted in the army. He was posted to Monte Casino in Italy where he was employed in the ambulance service dealing with the dead and wounded. We were all slowly beginning to fly the nest.

A short while after I'd stopped seeing Jimmy, I was told by one of the girls that their 'Big Sergeant', as he was known, had been asking questions about me. He was in charge of the parachute packing area where she worked, and his hanger was close to where all the girls had to pass in order to reach the ladies' toilets. Apparently, he had spotted me and was asking his girls questions about me. I was in the toilets when my friend Regina came rushing up to me. 'Ewa, our Big Sergeant's been asking about you, he wants to know if you'll go to the dance with him.' The dances were held regularly in the Sergeant's Mess Hall.

'No, I won't,' I replied. 'If he wants me to go with him he will have to ask me himself.' Another major factor was that I'd never set eyes on him so I didn't have a clue what he looked like. Later that day, after we had finished work, we assembled as usual to march back to our barracks. Regina nudged me and said, 'Ewa, that's him, that's him.' She pointed over to where a tall, good-looking man stood watching us. I was pleasantly surprised as he was, I thought, a cross between Errol Flynn and Robert Taylor who I'd always had a thing for. Things were looking up!

The next day, Regina told me he had asked her again if I would go to the dance and so she had relayed my message to him. On the night of the dance I was on edge hoping he would come and wondered if he would actually approach me. Suddenly, he appeared at my quarters. His name was Bill Pitcher.

Paths Cross

William Albert Pitcher was born on 25 February 1917 at 128 Addison Gardens, Shepherds Bush. Called Bill or 'young Billy' by his mother, he was the only child of William and Alice Pitcher. His father was born in Enfield and spent most of his youth growing up in West Ham. At the age of fifteen, he trained as an apprentice with the Great Western Railway, learning engine fitting and twining (steel cable manufacture). After a promotion to the drawing office, he moved to a similar appointment on the Central London Railway. There he was concerned with the building of the Underground at its onset. He was placed third in a national geometry examination and was awarded the King's Prize.

At the outbreak of World War I he served as a sapper in the Royal Engineers, fighting in France. He was involved in digging the trenches, but as a result he became seriously wounded. He sustained permanent damage to his eyes and spent a considerable time in hospital. Several years later he joined the Times Furnishing Company as a French polisher and remained there for twenty-six years until he retired.

Bill's mother was born in Sydney, Australia, and was the eldest daughter of a Swiss father and an English mother. Later, the family returned home to England where her father bought a hotel. Due to mismanagement of the finances by his business partner he was forced to sell up. He then eventually became a top chef working for J Lyons & Co. and the Cannon Street Hotel among others. Alice was sent to finishing school in Switzerland, along with her younger sister, May, and on her return worked as a milliner.

Bill always regretted being an only child and would have loved to have had brothers and sisters. He had quite a lonely childhood so he grew up being very close to his maternal grandparents. After junior school where he passed the eleven-plus examination, he went to St Clement Danes, but left at the age of fourteen to earn a living. He found himself a job in St Paul's churchyard and then worked as an invoice clerk for Cater Platt. From here he went to work for Alfred Dunhill before deciding he wanted to join the Royal Air Force.

He signed up for eleven years in 1935. After joining, he trained as a safety equipment worker and worked his way up until he was eventually promoted to sergeant. During this time he was stationed at Uxbridge, Cranwell, Usworth, Hucknall and Kent before being posted to Egypt. From here he continued on to Somali Land and Abyssinia where he worked in the No. 2 Repair and Salvage Unit. This unit consisted of twenty-five men plus two sergeants, Bill being one of them, and a Flight Sergeant. The Flight Sergeant was a trained motor mechanic and the only person able to drive. He proceeded to teach everyone how to drive a fifteen-ton truck where gear changing, either up or down, meant double declutching all the time. The Unit's first solo drive was to take fifteen trucks 1,500 miles from Abyssinia to Madagascar.

From here Bill was posted to the Eastleigh camp near Nairobi and put in charge of the Repair and Salvage Unit, which dealt with safety equipment. This included dinghies, floatation gear on aircraft and the making and packing of parachutes. The hanger he worked in was situated right next to where the Polish WAFs were working. Each day, along with all the other men, he would watch the Polish girls march past. His eyes picked out one girl and he thought to himself, *That's the girl for me!* Her name was Ewa Lugwiga Cisalowicz.

Love and Marriage

We went out on our first date and found we got on really well as we both felt very comfortable in each other's company. The conversations turned out to be a little more difficult as I could only speak a little English and some Swahili. Luckily, Bill was well versed in Swahili as he had twenty-six African tailors working for him, but he couldn't speak a word of Polish.

To remedy the situation we ended up carrying a translation book and, when necessary, would look for words that conveyed our meaning to each other, so all in all we managed to communicate reasonably well.

It was the start of our relationship and afterwards we continued to see each other on a regular basis. Every lunchtime we would meet up, eat our sandwiches and spend time together. On Saturday nights we went to the dance and then on Sundays caught the bus into Nairobi. We usually visited the Stanley Hotel for refreshments, then strolled in the park and sat on the swings. In the evenings we made our way to the woods, as did all the other courting couples. This was where all the love-making went on, but Bill never once pushed me into making love properly. He knew I'd had a very sheltered upbringing and told me later that he didn't want to risk losing me. It must have been very hard for him as we courted for eight months.

Two of the girls became pregnant and one of them had a quick registry office marriage. The other girl went back to her parents in the Masindi camp as the father of her baby was already married.

On one of our regular dates we were strolling around the town when we saw a church. Bill turned to me. 'That's the church where we are going to be married,' he said. That was my marriage proposal, but I didn't protest. He later gave me an engagement ring made of yellow beryl as this was about all you could buy at this time. Sadly, later on it was stolen.

Once we had decided to marry, I needed to obtain my father's permission to do so. We wrote to him explaining our intentions and he replied that if that was what I wanted, he was very happy for us. As all our personal documents were left behind when we were forced from our home, I didn't possess a birth certificate. I needed to swear an affidavit stating my date of birth. This was a written document made under oath before an authorised officer. As birthdays are not celebrated in Poland, I wasn't totally sure of the year I was born and erroneously stated it was 1924 instead of 1923. On completion of my statement it was forwarded to my father to confirm the details therein. Being a man, and probably also unsure, he failed to notice the mistake. It was only a lot later in my life that the error was realised. Bill also needed permission to marry from his Commanding Officer.

As ours was to be the first wedding between an English RAF man and a Polish WAF, the Polish Commandant and a representative from the Polish Consul were to attend. Once all the relevant documentation had been received we were informed we needed to be married by Palm Sunday. After then the only priest was being posted back to England so there would be no one else available. The wedding therefore was arranged to take place on Palm Sunday itself. The date was 2 April 1944.

As Bill was in charge of ordering the silk fabric used for making parachutes he was able to obtain extra to allow for my wedding dress to be made.

One of his Indian tailors, who normally worked on parachute repairs, offered to make the dress for me. He came and took my measurements and then busily set to work. I had no idea what style it was going to be so I just had to put my trust in him and prayed I would like the finished article. Bill took a trip to Nairobi and managed to purchase a veil and also arranged for our cake to be made by the Sergeant's Mess Cook. It had two tiers and on the top tier two small flags were placed crossing each other. One was the Royal Air Force flag and the other the Polish flag, compliments of one of Bill's workers who had offered to make them for us.

I chose six of my friends to be bridesmaids. They would wear their evening dresses – all in an assortment of colours. These were the dresses they wore to the dances. All the men would wear their best blue RAF uniforms.

At last, the wedding day arrived. I was very relieved and happy when I saw my dress and got ready to make my way to the church where Bill had previously told me we were to be married. He looked so smart waiting for me to join him.

The wedding service was really lovely and as we left the church the men formed a guard of honour. After the photographs were taken, one of Bill's officers kindly lent us his car and we drove back to the Sergeant's Mess where we enjoyed food, followed by dancing. Once the reception had finished we were driven to temporary rented accommodation we'd found for ourselves in Nairobi. This was the first time we were to be properly alone.

We didn't make love. Bill just held me and made a fuss of me. He knew I was nervous and inexperienced; also we'd had a long day, so he was happy to wait until the following night.

As I had now married an Englishman I automatically became a British citizen. This meant I was no longer allowed to reside in the Polish Camp, but I was still able to work there. Thus started a new chapter in my life. On one hand it was sad to leave my friends and I missed the camaraderie, the company and fun we had together, but it was also an exciting prospect when I thought about what the future might bring.

As Bill was now married he was able to move out of the Sergeant's Mess and we started looking around for some more permanent accommodation. We found some rooms a small distance from Nairobi and our landlady was called Mrs Yates. She had a son named Carr Hartley, whom we were introduced to when he visited his mother. His occupation was to be a white hunter which entailed him going out on safari to hunt and capture wild animals. He was a huge man with hands like shovels and he had two sons who were exactly the same as himself. In comparison, his wife was only a small woman, but she ruled the three men with a rod of iron. We stayed with Mrs Yates for six months, eating all our meals with her and often with her family as well. Between us, we came to the decision that as we were a fair distance from the camp we needed to find somewhere closer to live. Getting transport into work had always been a problem for Bill so we hunted around and found new lodgings with a French family just outside Nairobi. Bill managed to get a lift in each day with a sergeant who had also married a Polish girl.

I gave up my work in the camp and found myself a job in the local hairdresser's. My duties there were general cleaning, sweeping the floor, taking rollers out and sometimes shampooing client's hair.

One day Bill became ill and had to go to hospital. He had contracted dengue fever. This is an infectious tropical and sub-tropical viral disease transmitted by mosquitoes. Fever, rash and severe pain in the joints are some of the main symptoms. When I first went to visit him I didn't recognise him and walked straight past his bed. I was so shocked when I saw him as he didn't look at all like the Bill I knew. His face was swollen and he'd got two black eyes. Thank God he gradually got better and came home after a couple of weeks.

On another occasion, as we were sitting together chatting, I looked down at his trousers and noticed a knife-edge crease running down each leg. 'Look at that wonderful kant,' I said. This was the Polish word for a crease and was pronounced almost the same as the rude English word c—t. Bill's face was a picture. 'Shh, you can't say that,' he said. 'It's a very rude word in our language.' He whispered in my ear what it meant. Suffice to say I never used that word again.

As soon as we had married, Bill applied for a posting to take us to England. We had no idea how long this would take, but six weeks later authorisation came through for Sergeant Pitcher and his wife. Unfortunately, the troop ship which was to take us on the first leg of our journey to Cairo in Egypt was being used to transport prisoners. This meant that no accommodation was available for wives so I had to stay behind until a suitable ship became available. Bill arranged for part of his wage package to be paid into the local Post Office so I could have enough money to live on while I was waiting to join him. When the time came for Bill to leave we said a very tearful goodbye. We had no idea how long it would be before we saw each other again. After Bill had left I needed to report to the camp each morning to check if my posting had come through. During this time I made a friend called Daphne, who was Kenyan and, like me, had married an Englishman. It was a help having each other for moral support as we waited to rejoin our husbands.

Homeward Bound

On arrival in Cairo, Bill found he was stationed in a transit camp on the outskirts of the city. He was housed under canvas in large tents and was to spend a total of six weeks there.

Every morning and evening at eight o'clock he would check to see if a posting had come through for me to join him. He had hated leaving me behind and was worried sick I might not be able to come or that he may be sent back to England at any time. Much to his relief confirmation finally came through that at last accommodation was available for wives on a troop ship sailing for Cairo. When I heard the news I was overjoyed and Daphne and I prepared to leave.

The first leg of our journey was to catch a train bound for Mombasa. From there we would board a troop ship and sail to Suez then board another train for the last leg to Cairo. The troop ship was only carrying women and we were allocated a single cabin each on the lower deck. These cabins were very small and became very hot in the daytime so we spent most of our time on the upper decks.

A canteen provided all our meals, but as there was nothing to do, time passed very slowly. I hardly saw Daphne. Although she had a husband, she was a good-time girl and spent all of her time with members of the crew. Unfortunately, one of them was interested in me. He had ginger hair, a beard and chest hair which was visible at the neck of his very smart white uniform. He kept pestering me to have a drink with him in the canteen or to meet up in the evenings.

Being newly married I was obviously not interested, but he was quite insistent. At the evening meal I would keep an eye on him to see where he was. If he disappeared from sight I quickly took myself back to my cabin and locked the door.

Each evening there was a total blackout and the decks were in pitch darkness. I was frightened that if I ran into him and rejected his advances he might force himself on me or worse still, throw me overboard. The cabin was very hot and there was nothing to do, but at least I felt safe.

We spent over a week on the ship and stopped only once at Aden. It was a great relief when we reached Suez and were finally able to disembark. Here Daphne and I said a sad farewell as her husband wasn't stationed at the same camp as Bill.

Along with some other wives, I boarded the train which was to take us on the last stage of our journey. I was really excited at the thought of seeing Bill again, as I had missed him so much, but I also felt slightly apprehensive in case he wasn't there to meet me. I needn't have worried.

As the train drew towards the station I hung out of the window scanning all the faces on the crowded platform. The Big Sergeant, so tall and handsome, was there with a big smile on his face as he spotted me. We were so happy to be together again, the emotion was overwhelming. We grabbed hold of each other, kissing, laughing and crying at the relief of being reunited once more. He told me later that he had been scared stiff that I wouldn't be aboard, but as the train pulled into the station he had caught sight of me at the window, my long hair blowing in the wind.

We made our way back to where Bill was stationed. The wives were given accommodation inside the camp, but their husbands remained outside in the tents. We spent six weeks like this as we waited for the posting to take us back to England.

We were able to spend the days together so we used the opportunity to take in some of the local sights. We managed visits to the Dead Sea, the Sphinx and the Great Pyramids – all of which were very interesting and exciting.

At last, the news we had been waiting for came through and on Christmas morning 1944 we caught a train back to Suez where we boarded a ship bound for England. I found not knowing where I was going a little daunting. I knew nothing of the country I was about to make my home and could speak only a little of the language. I was leaving all of my family far behind and had never met Bill's family so I had no idea what they were like or even if we'd get along.

Although we were married, I'd only known Bill for a very short while and in that time we hadn't spent very much time together. In spite of all my uncertainty, I knew deep down that I could rely on him to love and care for me. I didn't hesitate in putting my total trust in him and he was never ever to fail me.

Once on-board the ship, the women were provided with cabins but the men had to sleep in hammocks strung up on the decks. As it was Christmas Day the wives were given a proper Christmas dinner but unfairly, the poor men had to make do with a slice of corned beef and a hard tack biscuit.

Every day we would meet up so we could spend some time together. Because of the constant threat of U-boats there was a blackout at night and every day survival practice was carried out in case of an emergency. Bill gave me instructions that if the ship was ever under attack I must find him because if we were going to die we would do it together.

One morning, to our horror, the alarm signal went off as a submarine was spotted in the area. We all gathered on the decks and watched, terrified, as the submarine surfaced. Thankfully it turned out to be British so we were able to relax again.

Our voyage was to last two weeks, after which we docked at Liverpool on a freezing cold January day.

Now new and totally different chapters of my life were about to start.

Life Changes Completely

Once our ship had docked at Liverpool we made our way to the station and caught a train bound for London King's Cross and from there we took the Underground to Shepherd's Bush. We then hailed a taxi to take us to Second Avenue in Acton, where Bill's parents lived.

We were both absolutely frozen. Having snowed, it was bitterly cold and we had no winter clothes to protect us. Coming from the heat in Africa to the cold in England was an awful shock to our systems. The only clothes we possessed were those we'd worn in Nairobi so we were completely unprepared for the conditions that awaited us.

We knocked on the door and it was opened by Bill's mother. She had known we were coming but didn't know exactly when that would be, and she was pleased to see us. Ironically, one of the first things she said was, 'If I'd known you were coming I'd have swept the step.' Typically English! Sweeping your step was very important then.

Once inside, cups of tea were forthcoming and Bill's grandparents came down from upstairs as they lived on the upper floor. After a lot of excited chatter it was decided to have kippers for tea. Having never set eyes on them before I thought, *God I hope I'll like them*, as they smelt awful and didn't look particularly appetising. I needn't have worried as I thought they were delicious.

A bed was erected in the upstairs sitting room and this was to be our temporary bedroom. I was made to feel welcome, but I was very conscious of everyone watching me and obviously trying to work me out. I found it all a bit of an ordeal for, as far as I was concerned, I was in a room full of total strangers, but they were very kind to me and seemed very nice.

Bill and I were on a two-week break so the first thing we did was go shopping and buy some winter clothes. The rest of the time we just relaxed and took it easy – when we were not being besieged by a constant stream of visitors. All Bill's family and friends wanted to see young Billy and his new wife.

Once our break was over, Bill had to return to work at the RAF camp in Hornchurch, Essex, until he was demobbed. I was required to do war work and this turned out to be coil winding for submarines, etc. in a factory at Gypsy Corner in Shepherd's Bush. As Bill's demob date got nearer, we decided we needed a place of our own to live. A neighbour told us that he had an aunt who was looking to rent out a place, so we went to view the property. It was a semi-detached house that already had a tenant, Mrs Stephenson, who occupied the first floor. We had a good look around and decided it would be ideal for us. Not long afterwards we moved in.

It was great to have a place of our own at last and a proper bedroom. After obtaining the consent and gratitude of our landlady Bill set to work adapting and modernising the interior.

When Bill's demob papers finally arrived, he found himself employment as a foreman joiner, working in a small workshop or out on site. Not long afterwards I found out I was expecting a child and our first daughter was born in June 1946. We named her Linda. Seventeen months later our second daughter Gillian, known as Gill, was born in November 1947 and seventeen months later, yet again, in April 1949 our third daughter, Marilyn, came along. We now had three daughters under three years old. It was hard work and money was tight but we were happy and did the best we could. Bill's parents helped us out when they were able to.

As the girls grew we didn't have the finances to buy many things for them. I would shop at the local market and buy lengths of material from which I could make dresses, etc. and Bill's mum would knit cardigans and jumpers for them. For toys, Bill painstakingly built three doll's cots, all exactly the same, and I made all the bedding for them. Prams and bikes were always second-hand. Bill would strip everything down, respray the frames and oil all the parts to make sure they worked satisfactorily and, when they were finished, they all looked as good as new.

A shed was erected in the back garden and either side of a path, which ran the entire length of the garden, Bill grew his prized carnations. It was madness really as when you have three little girls tottering up the path with their doll's prams, you spend a lot of time praying that they wouldn't end up among their dad's precious blooms.

We acquired a little dog which we named Judy and the girls would put a bonnet on her and push her up and down in their prams. She just sat there, as good as gold, and never moved.

As our daughters grew, we decided we needed a bigger place and we wanted to move to the country. We searched in the Buckinghamshire area and found a bungalow on the Uxbridge/New Denham border in an area known as Willowbank. Willowbank was basically a large island between the River Colne and the Grand Union Canal.

There were two ways onto the island: a metal footbridge which spanned the River Colne and a small road for traffic, which had the water running underneath it. Our new home was the last but one of the bungalows and about fifty feet from the back gate was a weir. The river flowed down from Denham, under the Western Avenue, forking at this weir to join the Grand Union Canal. At the back of all the properties we each had our own river or canal bank that ran down to the water's edge. It seemed like heaven to us and was a totally different environment from what we were used to. Most of the roads were named after trees; our road was called Lime Walk, then there was Willow Crescent East and Willow Crescent West, Poplar Road, Hawthorn Drive and Alder Road. Lime Walk was lined with white flowering cherry trees, which produced a spectacular profusion of flowers every spring. There were no kerbs beside the road, just grass verges and a water ditch that ran in front of each property, disappearing up and under each driveway. With only the occasional car driving past, it was our dream location in which to raise our children. In September 1954 we left Acton and excitedly moved into our new home. Our house was called 'Rumble Weir'.

Rumble Weir

'Bill must need his brain tested,' was the first response when Aunt May first came to visit our new home. I have to admit she did have a point. The gardens were totally overgrown with waist-high grass and everything else had been left to grow wild. The inside was not much better. The walls were covered in very dark wallpaper and every room needed modernising and redecorating. At the top of the stairs there were two rooms, the smaller of which had a chimney rising right through the centre of the floor. Both rooms only had one small window at each end so they appeared very dark and uninviting. The property needed a new kitchen, a new bathroom, heating and larger windows. At the back was a so-called 'conservatory', but it was actually a lean-to.

Aunt May did not approve, but the girls loved it! On the riverbank you would see herons, kingfishers, swans, ducks, moorhens and coots. The water was full of pike and shoals of sticklebacks, which the girls caught with my kitchen sieves. Frogspawn was easily gathered from the water's edge and if you lifted large stones, newts could be found hiding underneath. It was nature at its best.

Bill decided to leave his old job in carpentry and instead took a job as an insurance agent working for the Co-operative. We didn't have a car so he bought himself a small motorbike or 'pop pop', as we called it, to enable him to go out on his rounds collecting the insurance money. Some of this work was done in the evenings.

At weekends and every free evening he would change his clothes and get on with modernising the house. I always served as general labourer; we had to do everything ourselves because we couldn't afford to have someone else do it for us. To save money, we bought second-hand wood, removed the nails and then planed it down to the size we required. Gradually, as the years passed, the house was transformed and we never took a holiday until the work was finished. Because we didn't want the girls to also miss out on a holiday, they spent two weeks every year with Bill's parents, who had moved to Lancing in Sussex, and we would join them on their last weekend.

Later on we bought a small car which gave us a lot more freedom and for future holidays we went to Jaywick Sands, near Clacton in Essex. I can remember one year, just before we were due to go away, the girls all contracted chickenpox and were covered from head-to-toe in spots. We made the decision to go regardless, but ensured we walked a long way up the beach to be well away from everyone. The sea water did the trick and dried up the spots very quickly.

Time passed and before we knew it the girls had started school and had decided to join the Brownies. Each year an annual gathering of Brownies and Girl Guides was held at Lady Vansittart's estate in Denham village. The whole family would attend and to get there we needed to wade across the canal. This was possible because just below the water line a concrete shelf ran from one side of the canal to the other. This was where the river forked to join the canal. The river was quite shallow but the canal was very deep and was used regularly by barges and other motor crafts. From here we walked over the fields, across the Western Avenue and continued on to the village. One year Linda's friend Rosemary and her mother accompanied us. On the way home, having reached the canal, we removed our shoes and waded across. Rosemary's mother was last. She was a large lady and was wearing a grey plastic mackintosh. Unfortunately, the concrete shelf was slippery due to a build-up of algae and half way across she slipped and fell into the canal. Her coat billowed up around her and she floated slowly away on her back until she was caught by a mass of lily plants. We were all horrified but Bill just said, 'I suppose I'd better go and get her.' He took off his jacket and shoes, swam out and towed her back.

It was in the canal that Bill taught the girls to swim. The incentive was that when they swam the width they received half a crown (twelve and a half pence these days).

Life carried on as normal and, as the girls were all at school, I decided I would like to work, not only to earn money, but to get me out of the house. I found employment at lunchtimes dishing out the puddings in the canteen at Mac Fisheries. Later on I went to work for Commercial Ignition in Tatling End as a coil winder. My job involved sitting at a machine where insulated copper wire was wound thousands of times round a permanent bar magnet. This produced a solenoid which was used in submarines, cars, tanks and lorries, etc. I really enjoyed my job as there was great camaraderie among all the girls and I stayed here for a number of years.

Suddenly, out of the blue, Bill's father was kind enough to help us out financially. He dealt in the share market and always had his nose buried in the *Financial Times*. He owned a lot of Indian rubber shares and, when the price soared, he sold them and made a large profit. He gave us enough money to pay off our mortgage which helped us enormously and made life all the more comfortable.

The time spent in Rumble Weir was very happy and each year we had large Christmas celebrations to look forward to. Bill's parents always came to stay with us over the festive season and the girls would go carol singing. I occasionally would creep up the road in the dark to listen to them singing. They would sing a complete carol, before knocking on a door, and then sing another carol. Sometimes one of the girls would play on a recorder and it would sound beautiful. The neighbours told me that they would always look forward to the girls calling. With the money they earned they would buy some small presents. One year Marilyn was very excited with a scourer she had bought for me to do the washing up! She had liked it because it was silver and shiny.

Another thing the girls would do was to fill four socks with a Satsuma and a few nuts and add a box of Maltesers or chocolates they bought with their earnings. They would then lay them out for me, Bill and his parents to find on Christmas morning. On Christmas Day I would put the turkey into the oven and we would walk up the road to Vi and Alf Scudders house for drinks. Vi was a small thin lady who waited hand and foot on her husband Alf who was the complete opposite. He was very overweight and he would sit in his chair for a large part of the day. We would say Alf would never make old bones, but ironically Vi died a long time before he did and he was to live into his nineties. After we had finished our drinks we would return home for

Christmas lunch. We always had turkey with all the trimmings and it was only ever eaten at this time of year. This was followed by Christmas pudding, with sixpence pieces hidden inside, and a special treat of tinned fruit cocktail. Dates, nuts, figs, marshmallows, Turkish delight and stem ginger would round off the meal.

In the evening several of our neighbours would call in and we would play some games. Everyone's favourite was called corks. The corks were lined up down the centre of a table, one less than the number of people playing the game. Playing cards would be dealt out to all the players and on the word pass everyone would pass one of their cards, face down, to the player on their left and pick up the card passed from the player on their right. If the card received made a pair with one in your hand you made a grab for a cork. If you were unfortunate enough not to get one you would be out of the game. This would continue until a winner was left. This was a very popular game as it was always so much fun.

Time Passes

The years passed, the girls grew up, left school and found jobs. They would all regularly go out dancing on Saturday nights with their hair and make-up looking immaculate. Hours later, they would return home after a half-hour walk looking much the worse for wear. They would be worn out, their make-up and hair would be far from perfect and they would walk on the grass verges, carrying their shoes because their feet hurt.

Throughout the years many boyfriends came and went. Linda was the first to leave the nest. She met Brian, who also lived in Willowbank, and they married in June 1966, setting up home at Speen in Buckinghamshire. Gill married David in June 1969 and moved to Widmer End – very close to Linda, who had relocated to Hazlemere, also in Buckinghamshire. After a blind date set up by a friend, Marilyn married Ric in 1970 and went to live in Battersea in London with Ric's parents. In September 1971 they decided to move abroad, initially for two years, to Cape Town in South Africa. They enjoyed the life so much that they made the decision to stay there indefinitely.

Grandchildren were forthcoming. Linda gave birth to Kieren and Lisa; Gill to Mark and Christopher; and Marilyn to Lianne and Jason. Sadly, Bill's father never saw any of his great-grandchildren as he passed away in 1968, but his mother did. She moved to a flat in Uxbridge, Middlesex, to be near us and, with her help, in 1972 we purchased a holiday home in Pevensey Bay, East Sussex, approximately 100 yards from the sea.

Bill and I would go to our holiday home a lot at weekends and it became the main holiday destination for all the family. The grandchildren absolutely loved it! Bill kept a boat on the beach and would go out fishing with his mate Ernie or sometimes beach fished instead.

To give me more freedom and independence we bought a mini which enabled me to visit Linda and Gill after work. Bill no longer worked as an insurance agent and after leaving the Co-operative he had a variety of jobs. He had been a joinery technician with Jayanbee Joinery, a sales office manager with steel manufacturers Kayser Ellison and a representative for Bryce White. After being made redundant for the third time he was employed by Sanderson Fabrics, where Gill's husband David worked, along with Linda, who was David's secretary. In 1977 Bill retired early at the age of sixty and we came to the decision to leave Willowbank and move to Pevensey Bay permanently.

Bill's mother died in 1975 and she had left us her entire estate, which gave us the finances to live until we reached pensionable age. Another reason for our decision to move to Pevensey Bay was that our house had been burgled and all my jewellery stolen. After this episode we never felt the same way about the house.

We spent many happy years in the bay, coming back to visit Linda and Gill every six weeks or so. The family were always coming to stay and we spent hours on the beach or visiting the local attractions. A popular treat for the grandchildren was when Bill took them to Hastings to go boat fishing. Afterwards, he would buy them fish and chips in the Blue Dolphin café on the seafront. This was always the highlight of the day!

In 1979 Marilyn came back from South Africa with her two children when her marriage broke up. She moved in with us and Lianne and Jason attended the local school in Pevensey. Some years later the three of them moved to Aston Tirrold in Oxfordshire to live with Ric's brother David, who had a large detached house and needed a housekeeper. In time, things began to go wrong and Marilyn made the decision to come back to Pevensey Bay. While here, she met and married a man named Bill and they bought a house in Uckfield, East Sussex. Sadly, the marriage lasted less than two years. Lianne and Jason made the decision to go back to South Africa to be with their father. Marilyn then spent many years on her own, but in 2005 got married for the third time to Steve. They lived in a flat in Patcham, Sussex, to start off with and then bought a bungalow in Peacehaven, where they still are to this day.

Gill's marriage to David also floundered and they divorced in 1986 after sixteen years. In 1989 she married Mike and they continue to live in the same house in Holmer Green. Luckily, Linda and Brian have managed to stay the course.

In 1994, as Bill and I were getting older, we decided to move to be nearer to Linda and Gill. We found a house which was ten doors up the road from Gill and all the family helped us to clear the gardens and install a new kitchen and bathroom. Later, bedroom units were assembled and the house was totally redecorated. We stayed with Gill and Mike while the work was completed and were very pleased when we were finally able to move in.

Our time in this house was very happy. Everyone was always popping in and out and each year we had large family Christmas celebrations to look forward to. As we aged we needed to rely on the girls more and more.

Bill gave up driving so we needed ferrying to all of our countless doctor/hospital/dental appointments, etc. and Gill took on the household accounts, tax forms, hair/beard/nail cutting and Bill's weekly wash down. In 2007 he was diagnosed as suffering from dementia with lewy bodies (DLB). This gave him symptoms resembling Alzheimer's and Parkinson's disease. He had problems with walking, memory and bowel functions. He also suffered from dry macular degeneration in both eyes and was unable to read or watch television any more. Eventually, he slept for most of the day and we were warned that his condition would worsen and we would have to wake him up to feed him. It got to the point where I couldn't cope any more and the family came to the terrible decision to admit him into a care home in Bourne End.

The staff were lovely, but Bill was very lonely and unhappy as we had never been apart before. Gradually, he deteriorated and stopped eating. He made the decision to stop taking the medication that was keeping him alive and only to take his painkillers. He died on 20 January 2008. I miss him so much, but I had found it difficult to see him as he was, a mere shadow of his former self. My beloved Bill was cremated and his ashes were interred in our local churchyard where I will join him when my time comes.

A little more than a year after he died my house was sold and I moved in with Gill and Mike. I feel very fortunate to have been blessed with twelve great-grandchildren and Bill lived to see ten of them. I will always remember him with undying love as a great husband, father and grandfather. I am certain when I pass on, if an afterlife exists, my Big Sergeant will be patiently waiting for me, just as he did all those years ago.

Family Fortunes

After I left the Masindi Camp in Africa to join the Polish Women's Air Force, Romek also decided to help the war effort and enlisted in the army as a paramedic. He was posted to Monte Casino in Italy and worked as an ambulance driver, picking up the dead and wounded. When the war ended he went to Sheffield to be demobbed. He found work on a building site and drove the massive cranes used for lifting materials. He met and married a local girl named Dolcie and they had two children, Christine and Andrew. He remained in the area all his life. Many years later he contracted skin cancer and, after several strokes, died in 1990.

After Romek and I left the camp the rest of the family remained and conditions improved. Scouts and Beavers were established for the children and the camp expanded with the addition of another village, a high school, a commercial school (which taught subjects such as business studies and book keeping) and a residence for students who were sadly orphans and had nowhere else to live. A hospital was built at the foot of Mount Wanda and a church, in the form of a cross, was constructed. Everyone was involved in the brick-making for these projects which was overseen by my father. When the church was completed, he went on to work in a footwear factory where he worked his way up to be the manager. Sports clubs were formed and activities such as volleyball, soccer and boxing were available.

In 1945 the war ended. Life began to be problematic in Africa because the African people started rebelling against the British who were in charge of the colonies. Due to the instability of the area the decision was made that, as the Polish Army was now integrated into the British Army, my family would leave Africa and go to England.

They left for Mombasa in the latter half of 1948 and slept on the docks as they waited for a ship to start a new chapter in their lives. Sailing to Malta and Gibraltar via the Suez Canal, they docked in England and were transported to Eastmoor Camp near York in the north-east. Food was in short supply in post-war Britain so they were fed three times a day from a communal kitchen.

With the arrival of spring they set about looking for employment. Mietek found a job in the textile industry. He lived at Eastmoor for some time, but eventually moved to Huddersfield, two doors away from Marysia. Here he met and married Fela and they had one son, Richard. Fela had a sister living in Canada and their mother went over to visit her. On her return, Fela's mother persuaded her daughter and Mietek to emigrate there as well. So in 1968 they left and made a new home in Ontario. They enjoyed a happy life and would come back on frequent visits to see the family.

Sadly, Mietek became ill and was diagnosed with prostate cancer, but after treatment he appeared to be cured. Unfortunately, he later succumbed to leukaemia and six years later, in 2000, he passed away.

Hanka returned to England with the rest of the family and she too lived at the Eastmoor Camp. She later met and married Kazik and had two children, Kazik and Krysia. She worked for a while at the Rowntree's chocolate factory. In later years, Kazik Senior was admitted to hospital with bronchitis and while there he sadly died. Two years later, Hanka met and married Lawrence and, after living in Leeds, they made their home in York. Unfortunately, Lawrence also passed away following kidney problems and Hanka was left a widow for the second time. She died suddenly of a heart attack in 2002 with Marysia at her side.

Marysia was the first to leave Eastmoor Camp when she found work with Wimpy Brothers, the building company, as a canteen assistant. While there she met Stan who was working on a building site and they married in Cambridge eighteen months later. They moved to Huddersfield to be nearer the family. Stan found work on another building site and Marysia found a job in the textile industry. They had four children, Anna, Krysia, Eddie and Barbara. In later life, Stan's health deteriorated and he was diagnosed with lung cancer. It gradually spread to his throat and he passed away in 2000.

Marysia has a good circle of friends, known as the 'Merry Widows' and they meet regularly and go on holidays together. She remains in Huddersfield and we are in regular contact.

My parents lived either with Marysia or Janek, until they bought a house two doors away from him. My father found employment with the local council. When he became ill he was diagnosed with heart trouble and then with throat cancer. His condition was not helped by being a lifetime smoker and consequently he died in 1974. Following my father's death my mother's health slowly deteriorated and she passed away in 1977.

Janek, or Johnny as he became known, was the youngest and therefore was still required to attend school on arrival in Britain. He went to school in Huntingdonshire and, on leaving, trained as a motor mechanic. Deciding that it was not what he wanted to do, he turned up on Marysia's doorstep saying he wasn't going back and found alternative employment in the textile industry. He met a Yorkshire lass named Glenys, married her and made the decision to buy a grocer's shop. Johnny left textiles and together with Glenys ran the shop. Later on they decided to sell the shop and buy a small supermarket. Unfortunately, through ill management, they lost this business. They then borrowed six thousand pounds to buy another grocery shop, but this venture also failed. They were made bankrupt and Johnny returned to textiles.

Johnny and Glenys' marriage was childless and unfortunately, due to their circumstances, both turned to drinking in excess. Johnny began experiencing chest pain and he was diagnosed with heart problems. He died in 1990 of a heart attack, aged just fifty-three. Glenys died some years later from cancer.

Marysia and I are the only remaining survivors of our family and we are well aware that we experienced some very hard times in our early years. However, we feel blessed that the majority of our family survived to lead normal lives and give birth to new generations. There were thousands of people who were not so fortunate.

Lightning Source UK Ltd.
Milton Keynes UK
25 February 2011

168213UK00001B/23/P